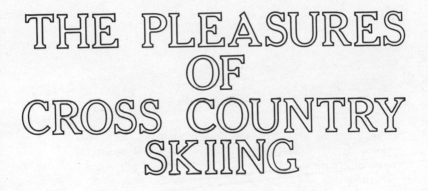

THE PLEASURES OF
CROSS COUNTRY SKIING

A bit of snow in a city park, open plains or farmland in winter, frozen lakes or mountain valleys and peaks are touring areas—all you need is snow. And when you get on the snow, go where you want to go at the pace you set yourself. Snow-closed roads cannot hold you. You will enjoy the quiet of an isolated cabin and the discovery of beauty. As they say in Norway, "God tur!" Good touring!

—*Ski Magazine*

Who Goes Ski Touring

People who are summer campers and hikers and are looking
    for something similar to do in the winter.
People who are looking for a gentle way to lead into
    Alpine skiing.
People interested in good, all-around, winter physical
    activity which is sociable and acceptable.
People who are just looking for an economical and safe
    way to ski and enjoy the snow.
Alpine skiers who have decided that long lift lines and/or
    the high cost thereof are no longer tolerable.

—Brochure from *Alpine Recreation,* Scarsdale, New York

THE PLEASURES OF CROSS COUNTRY SKIING

by MORTEN LUND

OUTERBRIDGE & LAZARD, INC.

New York
Distributed by E. P. Dutton & Co.

Dedicated to Norwegians,
who have kept alive the traditions
of the sport of ski touring
for all of us to enjoy.

Standard Book Number: 0–87690–077–5
Library of Congress Catalog Number: 72–84103
Copyright © 1972 Morten Lund
First published in the United States of America in 1972. Printed in
    the United States of America in 1972. All rights reserved including
    the right of reproduction in whole or in part in any form.

Design: Ellen Seham
         David Seham Associates

OUTERBRIDGE & LAZARD, INC.
200 West 72 Street New York 10023

CONTENTS

4. **Uphill and Downdale**

5. **The Outer Skier: Clothes and Equipment**

PRACTICING THE SPORT

6. **Jogging on Skis to Lose Weight and Improve Your Condition**

The author's father and mother skiing cross country in the accepted 1920's fashion.

ABOUT THE PEOPLE
WHO MADE THIS BOOK

Morten Lund is a freelance writer and filmmaker who has been skiing since age three and writing about it since age twenty-five.

The author's twenty years experience in the ski field easily ranks him among the most expert of ski writers.

His books include *Skier's World* (Ridge Press), *Expert Skiing* (Doubleday), *Ski GLM* (Dial Press), *The Skier's Bible* (Doubleday), *Skier's Paradise* (Putnam), *Ski in a Day* (Grossett & Dunlap), written for Clif Taylor, and *Adventures in Skiing,* written for Minot Dole. He has written outdoor articles—most recently for *On the Sound, Boating, Signature, Holiday, Travel & Leisure, Sport* and *True.* He is the former staff ski writer at *Sports Illustrated,* and is currently general editor of *Ski Magazine.* He directed two currently available films on ski technique: *Five Days to Ski* (Head Ski Corp.) and *Ski Touring is for People* (Garcia Ski Corp.).

Steve Rieschl, who worked with the author on the two chapters on teaching, has an outstanding ski touring program at Vail,

Colorado. The method developed by Rieschl, Sven Wiik, and their collaborators has the earmarks of the first American teaching method suitable for beginners in ski touring.

Rieschl, Wiik at Steamboat Springs, Colorado, Sverre Aamot of the Sugarbush Inn School at Sugarbush, Vermont, and the Trapp Family Lodge School at Stowe, Vermont, are all part of a growing legion of touring instructors capable of getting everyone out on touring trails all over this country.

The whole book had the help and critique of Michael Brady, *Ski Magazine*'s Nordic editor, a long-time resident of Norway and the only American member of the Norwegian cross-country racing coach association.

The winter outdoor chef chapter is wholly the work of Bea Williams, whose expertise in outdoor cooking extends to saltwater cruising and backpacking, as well as ski touring.

The cover photographs, the inside photographs at Vail, and all the sequence photographs of Rieschl are Barry Stott's work; Stott is one of the country's outstanding sports photographers.

Cross-country skiing is an ancient means of travel. The oldest known finds of skis, from marshes in Kalvtrask and Hoting in Sweden, date back to 2000 B.C. In Norway similar finds have been made in Ovrebo, dating back to 1000 B.C. The above picture of a ski runner carrying a bow is from a rune-stone at Boksta, Sweden, erected about 1050 A.D. (Source: *Finds of Skis from Prehistoric Time in Swedish Bogs and Marshes,* published by Stabslitografen, Stockholm, Sweden, 1950.) A similar carving on the island of Rodóy in Norway has been dated at 2000 B.C.

A touring skier sets off through the new snow.

CHAPTER I

The Esoteric Art
of Sliding
up the Mountain

A long time ago, a Nordic hunter on skis got too close to a big reindeer and was trampled. He was carried off; but his skis were left behind, embedded and preserved in a Swedish bog. The skis were discovered in the mid-nineteenth century when the site was examined by archaeologists. They determined that these skis dated back to 2000 B.C., the heydey of the Pyramids.

So, preliterate Scandinavians started it all long millenia ago: they had found a good way to get out to stands of firewood, to stalk reindeer, and to travel from one snowbound village to the next; they were not in the least concerned about going downhill as opposed to going uphill.

The earliest depiction of skiing is a sketch in stone which shows a proto-Finn pumping along on one long ski and one short. The drawing is called "Skrid-finnen" or "The Striding Finn." The short, fur-bottom ski acted as a pusher, like a man on a leg-powered scooter. Skiing it was. Beautiful it was not.

Touring History

The terms "cross-country skiing" and "cross-country ski touring," have often been used interchangeably. Cross-country skiing covers both cross-country racing and ski touring. If you want to distinguish skiing across the countryside for pleasure from the competitive sport then you should use "ski touring."

Modern American skiing has come a long way from its early simplicity. Since "downhill only" became the rage in the 1940's, U.S. ski resorts have become very posh. The big cable lifts installed in Squaw Valley, California and Snowbird, Utah for 120–125 people at a time cost $3 million. The sophistication of downhill skiing and its cost both accelerated. By 1960 almost no one practiced the simple walking on skis which began the whole sport of skiing.

The direct descendant of the early ski form of Scandinavians is ski touring, and it *is* beautiful. While millions of Americans and middle Europeans go plunging down from the upper terminals of their skyscraping, steel-girdered ski lifts, Scandinavians typically reserve their greatest energies and willingness for the still simple ski-walk-in-the-woods, requiring no lifts, no après-ski bars, and, best of all, almost no money. Even today, you can get outfitted for about $35 in Oslo, Norway's capital city. After that, the only thing you need is fifty cents for the Oslo subway that takes you up to the hills above town, and a few goat-cheese sandwiches to fuel your hike through the woods.

Ski touring is beautiful for its simplicity and for its lovely look—a free, swinging way of walking: soul, in Scandinavian.

In Northern Europe, ski touring continued to be an indelible part of history. The Scandinavians, unlike us, never let it die. When the Swedes fought their round-robin wars with the Norwegians, and the Norwegians the Finns, and the Finns the Swedes, they sneaked up on each other on skis carrying muzzle loaders. It was a tradition.

Back in the early 1940's, when Stalin decided to invade Finland, the Russians ran headlong into this tradition. They found themselves fighting an invisible army. Gunfire came bursting out of a blizzard followed by ghostly white specters on skis who annihilated tanks and men, then disappeared only to reappear ten miles away in a second strike. The Russians backed off.

Revival of Tour Skiing

In the 1800's and early 1900's, the old Scandinavian farms were being divided up among descendants whose numbers had increased tremendously thanks to modern medicine. Instead of birth control, they had America. Some three million Norwegians alone immigrated to the U.S.

But, on the blizzard-swept, live-or-die-by-your-guts plains of the old Northwest, the immigrant "Squareheads" had too much

Stott

Downhill on touring skis in Vail Pass, Colorado.

to do just surviving. Ski touring became peripheral. Even in the Midwest, touring has only now started to recover.

This year, one out of five pairs of skis imported into the United States came from Scandinavia—and most of these were touring skis.

A Beginner's Sport

There are probably a quarter of a million Americans learning to ski downhill-only each winter. Drop by while a novice class works out at one of the larger resorts. The pupils, by and large, start out scared.

Then look in at a class in ski touring: you'll find grandmothers, grandfathers, and children setting out confidently over level ground on soft, easy snow, or going out into good-looking country without any more strain than walking to church.

Ski touring is first of all a fine, gentle introduction to the sport of skiing as a whole. Scandinavian instructors prefer to see pupils learn a little touring before they take on the more difficult (for beginners) downhill or Alpine skiing, which initially requires more athletic ability. Downhill skiing means sliding at the mercy of gravity. You are tied to your skis, heel and toe. It takes a couple of years and a sprain or two before you learn how to keep from falling hard or hitting trees and other skiers on your way down.

The downhill boot is enormously stiff and heavy. The downhill ski weighs a ton. Bindings that nail the heel to the ski are strong impediments to walking. Coming back to the lifts after lunch, most skiers carry their skis across their shoulders. It hurts to walk on them.

Advantages of Touring

Touring, taught correctly, is a snap. Many tour skiers in this country never learn anything as sophisticated as the "diagonal stride." They simply walk on their skis. There is no ten dollar lift ticket, no necessary two-hundred-dollars-for-skis-and-boots. The tour skier can start out for $75. His outfit—light pliable boots, minimum weight skis, a binding that lets him lift his heel as in normal walking—weighs seven pounds less per foot than the downhill outfit. (Imagine each foot with an extra seven-pound sack of sugar wrapped around each ankle.)

The tour skier likes to travel with two or three or five people in the woods. His party may be the only group for miles. There's no shouting, no screaming or grinding of lift wheels. Miracle of miracles: it's quiet on a touring trail.

One winter Saturday this writer and two other tour skiers spent several hours skiing Ward Pound Ridge Reservation, a public park some fifty miles north of New York City. Our contemporaries were skiing that weekend on privately owned ski resorts, waiting in lift lines, and skiing downhill in crowds; we three had a leisurely four-hour ski-hike, saw only our own tracks, those of deer and rabbit, and met only one lone foot hiker.

One of our party, Bea Williams, had never been ski touring before this day, yet she managed to keep up with us quite well. Beginners can share.

Lift Skiing Gone Wrong

The four million "lift skiers" in this country outnumber ski touring enthusiasts by about twenty to one. A super image-building job has gone into making Alpine skiing (often a cold, demanding, competitive and difficult recreation) seem safer, more desirable, easier, more accessible and glamorous than it really is.

Consider a typical Alpine ski day: You line up your car in the parking lot, stand in a line to buy a lift ticket, line up at the lift, ride the lift in a line to the top, ski down the trail behind a line of skiers, then stand in line at the lunch counter to eat before you go out and stand in line again at the lift. You never leave the crowd.

There is a wait of thirty minutes or more at the best resort restaurants. Food prices are high. Ski towns are growing like crazy and weekly rent for good resort apartments is $350; a single cheap room at a premier resort like Aspen is $160 to $200 a month.

The land in and around resort areas is subdivided and re-subdivided for maximum profit. The anxious snobbery of the suburbs has been imported to the mountains. Footloose skiers who used to give resorts their vitality and spontaneity are being priced and policed off the slopes, making resorts affluent en-claves of the dullest stripe. Furthermore, grand circuses of ski trails now run for miles into the surrounding country, with their attendant steel pylons and machinery. The ecological impact is ignored.

Alpine skiing is now subject to the classic plagues of a con-sumer society. Newer, better, more expensive artificial materials pre-empt the old. Bamboo ski poles went out ten years ago, wood skis six, and leather boots three. Aluminum, fiberglass and polyethylene have replaced them. Good Alpine skis are now a sophisticated $150 to $300 mix of materials. Good Alpine gloves cost $15 to $20 a pair. The pressure to buy the best is terrific. A family of four outfitting itself with top Alpine equip-ment and clothes today runs up a bill of $2500 or more.

Touring as a Counter-movement

But the reaction is setting in: When Polly Specht of Niagara Falls went west a season ago to Mt. Werner in Steamboat Springs, Colorado to work at Scandinavian Lodge, she reported, "People are tearing up their lift tickets and going ski touring.

"We go out in the mountains and instead of meeting people we meet elk," Polly said. "You can stand on a cross-country trail looking back at Mt. Werner and see the people swarming down the hill like ants."

In *The Greening of America*, Charles Reich asks, "How could skiing be turned into real culture? The first requirement,"

Downhill into virgin snow in Colorado.

Reich decided, "would be that the individual choose freely to try the activity without the pressure of salesmanship, social prestige and image-fulfilling."

Reich's "Consciousness III" skier would definitely be a touring skier who has ". . . a greater proportion of activity to purchase of commodities" than the Alpine skier.

On our Pound Ridge trip, the expenses—for the two of us from New York—were $2 for gas and approximately $2.50 for food. We had a surfeit of peace for that price. We had the company of Bjorn Kjellstrom, at sixty years old a happy, fit man —a testament to the good effects of ski touring.

We had been completely equipped for ski touring at less than $75 apiece, including light, narrow skis, low-cut boots, wood poles, gabardine touring knickers, long socks and windbreakers. We did not need our heavy $80 down parkas for cross-country skiing because there is no lift ride to get cold on. The motion of walking kept us constantly warm. Our touring outfits weighed scarcely eight pounds apiece. We were touring at a third the weight and a sixth the investment needed for Alpine skiing.

The increasing popularity of touring has caused new products, synthetic and more expensive, to be marketed in the field. However, there is no *need* for expensive gear in touring. You can enjoy touring without super-products.

Tour skiing will remain simple because it embodies a philosophy as well as a form. The Alpine skier lives in an exciting world of a high speed sport with a heady night life. The touring or Nordic skier lives at his own pace, a "sweet speed." He heads for a nearby wood in an easy early-morning tour when the snow is crisp and yields the best touring. The Nordic skier finds it natural to make his own lunch of dark bread and unretouched cheese. He eats it sitting on a log and asks no one's permission to sit.

John Christie, manager of the Mt. Snow Alpine resort in Vermont, once commented, "It is just incredible. Our skiers seem to go looking for the longest lift line so they can stand in it." The most unnatural fate of an Alpine skier would be to find himself alone on a ski trail.

Kjellstrom greeted us at Ward Pound Ridge Reservation by himself. I told him that a friend of mine who had wanted to come had not been able to make it. Kjellstrom said, "Three is a good number." During the last mile or so, he drew away from the two of us, skiing on ahead. When we took off our skis, he said, "I skied ahead to give you a chance to ski by yourselves."

Touring needs no lifts, no motors, no wholesale tree cutting. It uses winding, narrow trails. Kjellstrom, with the help of the national organization known as The Ski Touring Council, laid out some twenty to thirty miles of trails at Pound Ridge along old farm paths. By clearing out brush, he turned thickets into nice walking paths for deer as well as skiers.

Older skiers concerned about ecology, as well as younger skiers whose ethic is against the heavy economic structuring that is now wound around Alpine skiing, have been turning to ski touring. "Ski bums" at Aspen go out and climb up the hill under the lifts and ski down on cross-country skis to avoid the $9 a day lift ticket. (Ticket prices climb and many resorts that used to supply the ski bums with lift tickets provided they worked at the resort, have now withdrawn the privilege.)

Tour ski sales are up 50% as of two years ago, 100% this year and Fischer, the biggest maker of Alpine skis in the world, has started making Nordic skis for the first time.

Touring and Snowmobiles

Gerry Cunningham of Denver, one of the country's leading specialists in mountain and winter equipment, said, "The snowmobiles have shown one thing: downhill skiing is not satisfying the nation's desire to get out in the winter because the people who don't ski are buying these expensive machines."

Ski touring may not have a hard time expanding because, in a sense, the tour resorts are already there. Almost every large Alpine ski resort and many individual ski lodges have already started ski touring. Steve Rieschl at Vail, Colorado often has forty to fifty people per day in classes at his touring school. The

Trapp Family Lodge School in Stowe, Vermont, frequently gets as many as the Stowe Ski School in mid-week. Sverre Aamot's school at Sugarbush, Vermont, gives 2500 lessons a year.

Still speaking about snowmobiles, Gerry Cunningham pointed out the need for ". . . something that's as easy uphill as snow-shoeing, and as much fun as downhill skiing, and easy to learn."

Ski touring is the answer. You can aim at any level of exertion you wish, from gentle walking to strenuous mountaineering. Ski touring offers you a chance to put yourself back into the rhythm of the outdoors, to participate in its tranquility in tune with the "slow pulse of the land."

Ski Magazine wrote, "Ski touring is not Alpine skiing where you are challenging the mountain. In ski touring you are challenging your perceptions. It's hiking through the woods on skis: a new way to be out there."

CHAPTER 2

Touring in the Fields

Ski touring on the flat is basically simple walking and sliding. A tour skier who learns in a field before he tackles hills is doing the wise thing.

Unfortunately, there are over-ambitious, eager teachers who have a thousand tricks to make even such a simple thing difficult. Bjorn Kjellstrom is against any instruction on the flat at all for the first few minutes. "Let them just walk around on the skis, then teach them. Don't make it complicated," he said.

The writer has seen many beginners pushed onto the hills without any field practice at all and nearly scared to death by the rolling terrain. To the beginner, a mild slope seems a precipice. It doesn't take much of a climb to take the heart out of a raw novice who has never skied. It doesn't take much of a downgrade to spill him. Beginners pushed too hard by being sent down hills they are not ready for are needlessly frightened by what is a simple sport.

The beginning tour skier needs, after he has conquered his flat field, a trail; but he needs one with very slack uphills (not more than 5°), gentle downhills, plenty of runout space at the bottom of any hill, and no sharp corners on the downhill parts.

A practiced tour skier can take terrain just about twice as fast as he could hike it, on the average—five to six miles an hour in a sustained tour of fifteen miles, so experienced skiers nearly always overestimate the ability of novices to keep going. What is as simple as walking to the practiced tourer is not for the beginner. He needs lots of stops.

Some teachers confuse racing techniques with ski touring techniques.

In top speed travel on extra-light skis narrower than tour skis, a cross-country *racer* can go *ten* miles an hour, mile after mile, showing a characteristic "kick up" of the tails of the skis as he goes. Cross-country racing has a different, much more extensive ethic, one that requires much more training time and hard work than ski touring.

Touring is a diversion, not a contest. The cross-country racer can be a very bad teacher: he is impatient to get moving and show his stuff, while the essence of touring is to take your own sweet speed.

Early Tour Terrain and Equipment

The beginner's vision of sailing across any and all terrain is an illusion: a beginner who starts on sidewalk-hard snow or two feet of untracked snow is a beginner in trouble. Tour skis will skid like hell on crust, and in deep snow they will seem to drag like lead canoes.

A first day terrain—and if possible, first day conditions—should be carefully picked; the training field should be worked on and cherished. It should be flat, and marked with a well packed-out double track, one for each ski. The track should be laid in a rough rectangle, a "box with slightly rounded corners" to give the beginner some experience in elementary turning.

Ski touring is *not* something anyone can embark upon with any old skis. Ski touring is deceptively simple, done with proper equipment, properly prepared. With bad equipment, it can be sheer drudgery. To invite people to learn to tour on Alpine skis is to wholly mislead them.

I was once trapped on the wrong kind of ski, when some friends of mine proposed a ski tour to the Taggert Hut up Castle Creek outside Aspen. I got to the rendezvous, horrified to find, too late, that we had been supplied with heavy heel-cable bindings and Head skis. Heads are fine for downhill but terrible for ordinary touring. No one had any wax. Unfortunately, Alpine skis are much too slippery to be any good in touring. It took hours to lead-foot to the overnight hut with five pounds of slippery Alpine ski on each foot. It was like hiking up a banana peel. We arrived exhausted after what would have been an easy tour on proper skis, properly waxed.

The tour ski should be a well-made, recognized brand. There are stores today that specialize in touring equipment (Alpine Recreation in Scarsdale, N.Y.; Scandinavian Ski Shop, New York, N.Y.; The Country Store, Aspen, Colo., to name a few.) There are several good touring stores in every state where people ski.

Touring Waxes

A proper ski needs proper wax. And the art of waxing is an art whose skills can be easily approximated but not easily mastered. The drier the snow, the harder the wax, is the rule of thumb. When the temperature begins to zoom above the melting point, it takes "klister," a sticky paste wax, to make the tourer's walk a sweet swinging stride rather than an undignified scramble. Waxing is just beginning to be appreciated in this country. Even experienced mountain skiers in America know very little about waxing.

Mountaineering, climbing-oriented skiers in the U. S. will strap "sealskins," real or simulated animal hides, under their skis to keep them from slipping backward on the uphill part of their tours. The accomplished ski tourer with properly waxed skis will walk right out ahead of the mountaineering skier on skins—except on very rare occasions, such as an opportunity to

Stott

Above: Two pupils striding on a flat at the Steve Reischl Ski School, Vail, Colorado.

Below: Touring past the traditional red barn in Vermont.

Carroll

climb a 45° wall of snow. The tour skier moves up with zig and zag and still gets to the top faster than the "skin artist."

The secret is in the wax. It has to be just enough softer than the snow under it so that as the skier's weight is placed fully on the ski, as the ski finishes its forward slide and presses down on the snow flakes, the wax will hang on the flakes with a firm grip. When the pressure is off, the ski glides forward again. Alternately pressing and sliding on his skis, the ski tourer performs the joyous miracle of sliding *up* a mountain.

Where to Learn

It is best to begin near home, if you have snow there—on a flat lawn, part of a golf course, a school football field, even a tennis court will do. And it is very important to pick a good day for learning. This means, first of all, not too warm. If it's too warm, your skis will stick (assuming that you don't yet want to fool with complicated waxing). The temperature should ideally be between 10° and 28°, never above 30°.

Most waxes, including the popular Swix and Toko, come in "green" and "blue" color codes for the below 28° range. Blue is the safest for all-around. You simply crayon some blue over the whole ski bottom. This will give you the approximate feeling of proper waxing.

In this temperature range (assuming there is no more than a mild wind) you will be comfortable walking around in a light sweater and a windproof jacket. You will find a down parka warm for touring in most temperatures, but, if you leave the zipper open when you move around, it will function alright.

If there's a hard wind, you will need either a down parka or a very heavy sweater under a windbreaker plus, possibly, "warm-up pants." A 25 MPH wind makes a 30° day feel like a 0° day. Cold. This phenomenon is called the "wind chill factor," and it's something most non-skiers don't experience for long: in today's society, it's usually easy to run inside whenever you get cold. When you stay out, you will really feel wind chill *working.*

A final requirement for a successful first day is the snow itself: The snow should be movable, like feathers or sand.

If the snow is solid crust or a soggy mass, you'll need a snow-mobile or trail grooming vehicle to crunch around on the practice plain until it *makes* a packed-down layer for you to ski on. If you can't do this, don't ski on the hard and shiny or soft and soggy. Wait for another learning day.

Starting Off

Every ski has a little toe binding to hold the boot toe down, and every little toe binding is either a right or a left. The toe-piece extends further out over the ski on the little-toe side. This is known as the "outside" of the ski.

If you have a heel-cable, as well as a toe-binding, the cable goes around the back of the boot; the latch that tightens the cable should be on the outside of the ski. If not, you are likely to catch the latches together and trip.

Walking around on skis is easy. Do it right away. You know how to walk, and you are on the flat, right? Just walk around and get used to the heft of the ski and its length. Don't go far, though. We want you back to teach you how to change direction.

The temperature is right, the wind is down, and the snow lies loose. You should take about 10 minutes to learn to manoeuver the skis at a standstill and another 30 to learn to glide properly during the first day.

Whether you are going to teach yourself, as this book is designed to help you do, or teach others, as this book can be very helpful in doing, you have to practice proper psychology. Strike a golden mean between skiing for hours without *any* formal exercises, and starting exercises *immediately,* without any fun first.

The First Minutes

Your first little space walk: you want to form the sides of a rectangle with your track, a "box with slightly rounded corners." This makes a track for your "gliding exercises," You will need the track to keep your skis going straight.

"Scooch down" into a half kangaroo stance. The scooching position is the same you'd take if you were walking over uneven or slippery terrain. It will help you maintain your balance. It is not a "sitting position" with fanny protruding because that will throw your weight too far back for good balance. Bend the knees forward and keep the hip bones directly over your boots.

Now, slide your skis flat on the snow, staying down at about seven-eighths of your normal height, doing a Groucho Marx sneaky walk. It's fun.

Slide, slide. Don't pick the skis off the snow at all.

Now you are ready to make the track.

Walk with the skis about twelve inches apart, and make a closed-circuit railroad track about a football field wide and half a field long, if you have that much space. These will be your gliding-training tracks. Use the poles to steady yourself as you go. When you come to corners, push off from the outside ski and step the inside ski inward. This is a "step turn."

The Book's Exercises

Now you are ready to look at the first exercises, which involve learning to manoeuver your skis at a standstill. You have already found that everything which involves a change of direction is harder than pushing skis straight ahead. We want to make it easier for you to change direction.

The step by step teaching exercises that follow are taken from a pioneering A-to-Z teaching method developed under American touring conditions. One of the chief developers, Steve Rieschl, who operates his own touring school in Vail, Colorado, demonstrates here and in Chapter Four. Rieschl's collaborators, a group of dedicated tour instructors in the American Rockies, have as an eventual aim national certification for tour instructors, both to promote the exchange of information and to set standards on instuctor apprenticeship and methods.

This book is the first publication of detailed sequence pictures of an American approach, from putting on the pole strap (opposite) to the wedel turn in deep powder. Yet this book is not intended to be a teacher's manual outlining all possible variations. Known exercises have been omitted for the sake of maintaining the pace of the book.

Interesting, as a footnote: the snowplow and stem turn sequences in Chapter Four are modelled on those in the 1971 American System for Alpine skiers. The American System from 1972 onwards is now de-emphasizing the plow and stem forms. Tour skiing, due to its free heel bindings, will always be dependent on the stem forms, and will preserve the classic stem turn for posterity.

Putting on the poles. To begin, put on and hold the pole properly. The strap of the pole is meant to support the hand. Therefore, you must put your hand through the loop from underneath and then grasp both the strap and the pole between thumb and forefinger. The strap takes the strain. Do not squeeze the pole. Hang in the strap.

Turning the tips. One of the first things to do after putting on the skis is to point them in a different direction than you started with. The simplest way is to step first one ski tip (below) in the desired direction and then the other. Repeat, making each step a swing of about two to three feet at the tips. You must pivot the ski *at the tail,* so that the tail stays in the same place. If you pivot at the middle of the ski, you will cross the skis' tails and be unable to continue.

Turning the tails. It may not always be convenient to turn the tips (say the tips are next to another skier). Turning the tails is also useful if you are on a slight incline because you can insert the poles in the snow to keep from sliding forward (top) as you shift your tails. Again, step one tail about three feet to one side. Follow with the other tail. You *must* pivot the ski from the *tip*, or you will cross the tips and be unable to continue your turn. Step first one tail and then the other until you have swung to face the desired direction.

Getting up from a fall. You may fall early or not at all the first day. It is not serious at any rate, because the heel is free to come off the ski. The kind of twist injury that occurs in Alpine skiing, where the heel is tied down, is almost nonexistent. The touring shoe bears the strain of any twist-force in a fall, not your ankle or knee.

The first thing to do when you fall is to swing the skis and legs so they are *on the same side* and your skis point in the same direction (top).

Then, get up on one knee, pushing with the hands (top left). Next grab the poles just above the middle and use them to steady you as you get up on both knees. Kneel between the skis (second from left). Now get up on one foot by shoving that ski forward. From that position you can use the poles to push yourself into a standing position.

The kick turn for reversing direction. As you get used to the heft and length of your skis, you may want a quicker way of turning completely around, a manoeuver that takes a dozen steps via the tip or tail turning method. So you try the kick turn. To start a kick turn, first decide which way you want to go. Swivel your upper body in the new direction a bit. You will now be facing one of your poles. Take that pole, insert it close to the tails on the far side of the skis (top left). Plant the other pole about halfway back along the tips, a couple of feet away on the far side of the skis (left).

Lean against the poles, using them as supports without moving them from the spot they have been planted in; "kick" the ski on the near side up in the air, so it rests on its tail in the snow (second from left). Then let the tip swing in a gentle arc until it lies on the snow pointing in the new direction (third from left). Finally, with poles still in place, pick up your other ski and swing it around in a half circle so it matches the first. You've made a kick turn.

Stepping around a corner.
Before learning how to
make time on the straight-
away, learn how to turn a
corner efficiently. Your
practice track is a rectangle. Here's the way to turn
the four corners: When
you come to a corner, stop.
Pick up the inside ski
(top right) and swing it tip
first about halfway to the
new track. Then put it
down and bring the other
ski next to it (opposite).
Then step the first ski all
the way into the new track
and bring the other ski
alongside (right). You're
on the next side of the
rectangle. All it takes is
six short steps. Don't
hurry them. Pretty soon
they'll be automatic.

Skating around the corner. By the time you have learned to go around the practice rectangle quite fast, stopping at each corner to step turn is a slow-down. Here's how to skate around a corner without slowing down as much. In the "exploded view" of skating around a corner shown here, the skier, reaching the corner, steps off with his inside foot without slowing down, puts the inside ski down and while gliding on the inside ski, pulls the outside ski (second picture from left) alongside. He then steps with the inside foot again and brings the outside ski over to it (bottom) until he has made it around the corner and is going off at right angles to his first direction. Skating is one of the most useful manoeuvers to master. It teaches the motions involved in turning on the hill. Try to skate each corner rather than stepping. Keep your speed up. Make the steps quick and short.

Learning to glide. It is entirely possible to spend your touring career moving along in a sort of shamble-on-skis. The difference between an efficient tour stride, which carries you twice the distance for the same effort, and a shambling walk on skis, is the *glide*. The glide is best learned with your poles *off*, because the glide should be powered largely by the legs, not the arms. Presumably you've waxed your skis: this means that you can shove off from one ski and "step" onto the second one (second from right). Right now hold it on the second ski! Freeze for a moment (third from left).

The momentum of your step will carry the second ski into a glide. Wait for the glide to take you as far as it can without slowing down. When it slows down, you step the next leg forward (third from right). Hold it. Glide (fourth from right).

The whole process of step-and-glide, step-and-glide is facilitated if you consciously keep knees bent so you are lower than your straight-legged normal height. This gives you better balance in a more flexible position, as well as a longer stride and a more powerful glide.

Gliding on the whole foot. In order to glide well and control the gliding properly, load your weight onto the gliding ski on the whole foot. The exercise shown here is an exaggeration of the proper movement but, nevertheless, is well worth doing to get the right feel. The skier should glide with his weight mainly on the gliding foot (fourth from right). In order to facilitate this, the skier lowers the hips and straightens his torso to vertical as soon as the glide gets underway and holds this position as long as the glide lasts (fourth and fifth from right).

Using arms for quick glide steps. A beginner can fall into the trap of overemphasizing the glide. There *is* glide with each step, but it varies with the pitch, the snow and the individual. Once you have gotten the knack of a good long glide, you should practice a quick short glide, like the one shown here, with bent arms. (You should be starting to think about arms, too). The natural arm motion of running (left arm and right foot ahead, then right arm and left foot) and a quick-striding minimum-distance glide will integrate one glide-and-stride with the next in a flowing movement. You want to end up with a stride where each given movement blends smoothly into the next. This is the exercise to do it.

Straight arm thrust with glide. Now it's time to add the supple-
mentary power of the poles to the "kick" of the legs to get the
maximum thrust to your skiing. The pole's power stroke must
fit into natural stepping-and-gliding. Keep the normal "walk
movement" you've had but swing the arms straight out in back
and in front in an exaggerated arc, so they come up over the
shoulders (top, second from right) as you stride. It's like fast
speed-skating. This long arm swing gives you a feeling for the
long elegant thrust of the pole.

Look again at the picture sequence at the bottom. Note how
the center of gravity stays between the skis, and the arms swing
straight along the track. Another insidious form fault is liable
to crop up at this point: Instead of proceeding with your weight
between the skis, and your arms swinging straight back and
forth along the track, you are liable to let the arm motion throw
you, so you end up, wrongly, with your head (and center of
gravity) wholly over first one ski and then the other (two il-
lustrations opposite, facing page). The weight should shift toward
the gliding ski but the body does not shift *over* the gliding ski:
It stays between the two skis. You spring *toward* the ski and
rebound.

An exaggerated side-to-side shifting of the skier plus a swing of the arm *across* the body rather than straight *down* the track wastes a lot of energy and throws you out of the track (above). Don't believe any book or teacher who insists that the body should shift over one ski and stay there for the whole glide. This "static shift" is a concept that counteracts the naturally fluid movements needed for a good stride.

Pushing with the pole. Now pick up your poles again and put them on. Carry the pole, thrust it into the snow and push off from it in coordination with the kick. Each time the pole goes back in the push-off motion, your hand must relax, so the pole is held not in a tense fist (upper picture), but in a relaxed manner between thumb and forefinger (lower picture), so the strap takes the brunt of the pushing motion. If you make a fist, you'll tire your arms much more quickly.

Gliding with the pole thrust. This exercise puts the "kick" of of the thrusting leg and the thrust of the pole together at last. The whole thing has to be as coordinated as a normal, but slightly exaggerated, walk. In the first picture, the skier is bringing the far leg forward. As it reaches forward, the near arm has pulled forward, as in normal brisk walking, and gently "plants" the pole, which has naturally pendulumed forward. As the skier now pushes the *near* ski forward and glides on it, the near pole is thrust back, handle going low past the hip, rather elegantly, not with a hard shove.

You must keep pushing on the pole as the arm swings all the way back. But the thrust is never hard, explosive.

A beginner often tries to make his poling motions short violent thrusts. The pole motion should be a long, even one, with the pressure on the pole continuing to the last possible second when the pole is far behind the skier. However, the push of the pole is not primary. The legs do the explosive powering. Note how relaxed the skier's hands stay. This is the classic "diagonal stride" of touring, so-called because one could draw a diagonal line across the body from the rearmost leg to the foremost hand. If you have trouble coordinating, simply start out in a normal walk, dragging your poles. Swing the arms as in walking. You'll soon have the right timing of hands and feet. Now, instead of dragging the poles, stick them in every time they come forward.

CHAPTER 3

The Ski, The Wax, The Day

Waxing.

This is a very complex subject, though we have treated it as a very simple one up to now.

On a short tour of a few miles or so, perfection in waxing isn't really crucial. On a day-long trip, a good wax job can be the difference between a back-breaking tour and one that is pleasantly exhilarating. The tour skier who does a little better wax job gets a much smoother kick-off and a much smoother, speedier glide. He climbs much more steadily without back-slips.

Why Wax Works

Let's recap what we've said so far. A layer of blue stick wax, used in below-freezing temperature, will do the trick. Add another layer for better results if the temperature rises.

The reason wax works or doesn't work lies in the nature of wax and snow.

Snow falls as hexagonal crystals with a set of arms extending from the main body of the crystal. Flakes underfoot consist of a bundle of several interlocked crystals. The arms of all the interlocked crystals in the bundle extend out to the sides so that it looks like a bristling hedgehog.

The snowflakes' bristles penetrate the wax on the ski bottom a little way as the skier presses his weight downward for the kick. This gives the ski its grip. When the ski is moved, the waxed bottom withdraws from the points of the crystals so the ski slides on. The same coat of wax, if it is the right wax, will cause the ski to grip and to slide. (This is something non-tourers find hard to believe.)

There are several quite different general snow conditions each calling for a different wax to ensure proper penetration. Too little or no penetration gives you a slippery ski (it won't hold), and too great a penetration gives you a sticky ski (it won't glide, because the bristles penetrated so deep they won't pull out: then snow clogs the ski).

The bristles of snow tend to shorten and round off with the passage of time, and do not penetrate wax as well. As snow ages it also tends to absorb moisture from the air. The edges or bristles soften. Snow has the tendency to thaw and refreeze into hard-kernel corn snow or an icy sheet. This reduces the bristles to nearly zero.

All three processes—rounding off, collection of moisture, and freezing—work to soften and stunt the snow and call for increasingly softer ("warmer") waxes. Only careful matching of the softness and depth of wax to the particular kind of snow makes a perfect ski that glides like a skate and grips like a vise.

In a minute we will go on to consider the kinds of waxes. But before we do, we need to prepare the bottom of the ski to receive the wax.

Two Kinds of Skis

There are basically two kinds of touring ski bottoms today: plastic and wood.

Lund

Bea Williams applying klister.

Plastic-base skis do not generally hold wax as well as wood. Some plastic bases will hold wax fairly well without much preparation in some conditions. Others need a "binder" for the running wax. Read the manufacturer's directions. The whole field of plastic touring ski bottoms is in a period of experimentation which will, hopefully, reduce their resistance to holding wax.

Wood skis have either a birch or hickory base. Either wood definitely has to be "treated" to hold wax well. To prepare the new wood ski, sandpaper off the protective coating that the manufacturer has put on. If the ski has been used, remove any old wax—you can use turpentine, gasoline or alcohol, but use these flammables in open air.

Treating Wood Bases

The very best way is to melt in a layer of pine tar or tar-like "base." This tar base is a protective coat for the ski as well as a binder for the wax. Untreated wood skis will soak up moisture.

To "warm in" a tar, you'll need a small butane or propane torch. These days most hardware stores carry small propane torches and a specialty camping store should have miniature butane torches that weigh only a few ounces. Either type will give an adequate flame. (The Soudoski, for example, is compact and convenient to take with you.) The tar preparation should be spread on like a thick paint; use a short, natural-bristle brush. Then, move your flame back and forth over a small section until the tar bubbles slightly At this point, move on! Bubbling tar means the heat has opened the wood pores and the tar is soaking in. No need for more heat. The trick in "warming in" a tar base is to keep the flame moving over the ski, never letting it stop. This way you will not burn the wood. The tar itself may flame briefly, but it will go out by itself.

When the first section has been "bubbled," wipe these inches clean of all excess tar with a rag. Bubble the next section. Wipe. Repeat until the whole ski is done. Wipe off all the tar that has not penetrated; you should be left with a *treated* wood ski bottom which feels dry or at most only slightly moist. If it feels really tacky, you didn't wipe off with enough force.

Applying hard wax on a tour.

Sometimes warming-in will cause the skis to take on more of a "bow" or arch than they originally had. If you see the skis have done this after you have finished both skis, tie them together at the middle, so both are flat. Then gently heat the middle of both ski tops and leave them tied for a day. When you untie them, they will take their original shape.

A single proper tarring ought to last a beginner a whole year of skiing. Warmed-in tar holds waxes better than anything else. You won't have to wax as often, either. Some beginning skiers find the whole tarring process a bit too much shopwork for their taste. They use a spray-on or paint-on base preparation. These bases wear off more quickly than warmed-in tar bases, but some skiers find these paint-on or spray-on bases perfectly satisfactory.

Wax and Snow

Don't panic if the detailed discussion that follows bores you. Just skip it and come back later when you've toured some. You can always continue to do what we've suggested up to this point—simply use a hard blue wax. Your skis will be quite slippery above freezing and you'll have to herringbone your way up the hill, but so what? A beginning tour skier is in no hurry, anyway.

Wax comes in three forms: a hard stick, a softer stick and a paste. Each wax form works best in certain snow conditions.

The three forms of waxes are:

—a "hard stick-wax" simply called *hard wax* (usually coded green or blue).

—a somewhat softer stick-wax called *klister wax* (usually coded red, purple, violet or yellow) yet, technically, a "hard wax."

—a very sticky paste wax called just plain *klister*, that comes like toothpaste in a tube (usually coded blue, red or violet). This is a "soft wax."

These three forms of wax are mated to five major snow conditions: 1) loose fine-flake snow (below freezing) ; 2) loose, coarse-grain snow ("corn snow" below freezing) ; 3) sticky snow (near the melting point of snow); 4) sopping wet snow (well above the melting point) and 5) crusty snow, or sheet-ice snow (once well above the melting point but now refrozen to resemble a crumbling "ice-cake" or a solid slab of sidewalk underfoot).

The three kinds of waxes are easy to identify by their containers; it's harder to identify the five kinds of snow.

Condition 1 = cool snow in fine flakes.

Condition 2 = cool snow in grainy corns.

Condition 3 = partly melting snow.

Condition 4 = wet spongy snow.

Condition 5 = hard slab crust or ice.

Identifying Snow

There are two tests to ascertain which kind of snow you have. The first test: carry a thermometer and stick it into the snow. Snow below 30° is cold, fine-flake snow (condition 1) or grainy corn snow (condition 2); snow between 30° and 34° is transition snow (condition 3); snow above 34° is wet snow (condition 4). If you can't stick the thermometer in, you have icy slab snow (condition 5).

(Snow temperature, incidentally, is not the same as the air temperature which your outside thermometer measures. The air temperature may be above freezing while the *snow* temperature is still below freezing, and this is a critical difference.)

The second way to ascertain snow type is to pick up and squeeze a handful. If the snow crumbles and can be blown away like feathers, it is cold fine-flake snow (condition 1). If it blows like grains of sand, it is cool corn snow (condition 2). If it can be partly packed and yet stays partly loose and can be blown away, it is transition snow (condition 3). If you can squeeze it into a perfect snowball, it is wet snow (condition 4). Crusty snow (condition 5) is easy to distinguish—it either has to be pried out as crumbling slabs, or it forms an ice sidewalk under your feet (without having been packed).

Don't be fooled into mistaking loose snow for icy, cement-slab snow simply because it has been packed down by skis or grooming rollers on a ski trail. Packed loose snow can be easily pried up with a ski pole tip, whereas "boilerplate" or "ice cake" cannot. Packed snow is either cold snow, transition snow or wet snow, and should be waxed for accordingly.

Practical Waxing

The best way to go at learning to wax is to start learning in fine-flake snow. Stay away from warm or re-frozen snow conditions until you have gotten your stride down and have had a chance to get some waxing experience. Happily, most of the early winter the snow will be cold, fine-flake snow and happily this mates to the hardest waxes (coded green or blue) that are the easiest to put on, take off and adjust for the various conditions.

Start your wax training with one little stick or tin (it looks like a short, fat crayon) of green or blue wax. This wax should be cool when applied, but is best applied indoors, where it goes on

---

Here's how the three waxes match up to the five snow conditions:

Loose, fine-flake snow, which we will call "condition 1," mates to a stick of blue or green hard wax.

Cool grainy corn snow, "condition 2," or warm flake-snow, near melting, also called transition snow, "condition 3," mate to a stick of klister wax.

Loose wet snow, "condition 4," or crusty slab snow, "condition 5" mate to a tube of klister paste.

Carroll

Corking hard wax to a shine.

better. Simply crayon green or blue wax on the ski and then use a rubbing cork—a flat, solid cork box which any touring store will sell you—to smooth the wax over the entire running surface. Use a little elbow-power on the cork and polish the bottom until it shines a little.

Let the skis cool standing up outside for 30 minutes before you use them. If you try to ski on warm skis, the wax will pick up gobs of snow.

Do not lay them bottom-down on the snow to cool. The wax will absorb moisture from the snow and ice up right away.

For re-waxing on the trail, the ski must be thoroughly dry: wax on top of water won't hold. You can dry the ski with a non-shedding cloth, but the easiest, quickest way is to carry a torch and fan the flame quickly over the bottom to dry it.

If it is very cold outside and you are on a tour with no indoor heat available, you may have trouble getting the wax to crayon on smoothly; the rubbing cork may not polish well either. You can use a torch to warm the wax in. First crayon the wax on rather thickly, then very carefully apply heat. (The wax should be barely warmed, *not* boiled.) Warm wax is easy to polish with a cork.

Another way to wax on tour is to use a waxing iron which also work wonders in cold weather; the waxing iron burns solid fuel pellets inside, or can be heated up with a torch. Simply run the hot iron over the thickly applied wax and spread it evenly.

De-Icing

After even the best of waxing jobs, ice can form under the skis in snow conditions 3 and 4, and ice can stop you dead. Ice usually forms first in the groove, so rub some paraffin stick-wax in the groove: paraffin never freezes up. And always carry a bar of paraffin with you.

Sometimes if you are icing up you can simply scrape ice off your ski and continue. This means you hit a local condition. But sometimes ice persists. If you are skiing cold new snow on top and breaking through to much warmer snow underneath, you will ice up continually. In such a case, you are in a quandry. Two different kinds of wax are called for at the same time: a hard wax for the cold top snow, and a klister-wax for the warmer snow underneath. Since usually you can't put on both at once (although it may be possible—see the part about combining waxes at the end of the chapter), the best thing to do is to scrape your skis and rub on paraffin over the whole running surface. This will give you a pair of de-iced but very slippery skis. You'll have to herringbone up the hills but you will make it home before dark.

To summarize: the complete tour skier has to cope with the conditions he'll meet up with using four forms of wax: paraffin bar, hard stick-wax, klister stick-wax and plain klister paste.

Advanced Wax Training

On a cold day (14 above or colder) when there's loose snow, begin by putting on one thin layer of green, the hardest wax. A thin layer of green, if sufficient, is more efficient than two layers of green.

Walk the ski not less than 20 minutes: wax needs to "mature" by use. If it grips and slides well at the end of 20 minutes, then everything is okay. If it starts to slip as you kick off, apply another layer of the green. If that doesn't work, put a "kicker" or thick layer underfoot. If the ski still slips, go to the next "warmer" wax in the hard wax series, blue wax.

If you start with a hard wax you can build layers of increasingly softer stick-wax without removing the under layer. But usually you cannot successfully apply a harder stick-wax on top of a softer stick-wax.

The system therefore is to wax for the coldest, hardest snow that you think you have. As the day warms, add another layer of the same wax, then apply the next warmer wax in the hard wax series.

It is better to err on the side of hardness. If the wax is too hard, you won't grip well; but you can always live with that for a little while if you have to, by side-stepping or herringboning up the hills. However, if the wax is too thick or too soft, the snow will stick to the ski as it slides forward, preventing the ski from sliding well. And you can't live with a ski that won't slide.

Klister Wax Use

Any klister wax will work fairly well with corn or transition snow (conditions 2 or 3). Klister wax is your third tin of wax, a hard stick of purple or yellow, depending on the brand, softer to the touch than green or blue. (Avoid using red klister wax. It only works for very special conditions.)

Klister-wax should be warmed when applied. Put it on thin at first. Dab it on, spread it thin with a scraper. You can polish it with a waxing cork. Speaking of waxing corks, there is a kind that leaves fewer crumbs—make sure you have that kind when you go to yellow or purple klister-wax because, unlike blue or green hard wax, it retains crumbs. The best cork is "expanded styrofoam."

Rub klister-wax in with the heel of your hand, if you have a cork that crumbles.

One layer of klister wax may not suffice: add another thin layer. Putting it on too thick in the second layer may result in a ski that clogs, and then you have to scrape the ski and start over.

Now, we've talked about snow conditions 1 to 3 adequately matched by three stick-waxes:

—(1) Cold, loose fine-flake snow—hard wax (green or blue)

—(2) Cold corn snow—klister wax (*not* klister paste)

—(3) Clogging transition snow—klister wax.

Use of Klister Paste

Conditions 4 and 5, loose wet snow and crusty icy snow mate to wet snow *klister* (purple), that very tacky paste that comes in a tube and squeezes out like toothpaste. Klister works great for condition 4: wet, spongy snow. A purple klister situation is a hot April day when the snow has turned to semi-mush under an Easter sun, or an overcast day with a constant drizzle. But when you use klister you will suffer a little for the advantage gained, because it is a somewhat difficult material.

Klister must be applied with care. Before beginning, run a paraffin bar down the vertical sides of the skis so that any klister that dribbles down can easily be pulled off.

Klister will not flow on well when cold. Keep it warm. To facilitate things further, you might squeeze a bit into a pot, heat the pot, and then paint it on with a brush. (This is a good method if you have three or more pairs of skis to treat.) You may heat the klister tube slightly with a torch, re-heating as necessary to keep it flowing.

If you apply klister from the tube, the normal method, squeeze it on in an interrupted zigzag pattern on each side of the groove, then smooth it out with a scraper, or better yet, with a wax iron. Klister needs only to be spread, not polished. Keep it thin.

Be prepared to clean the scrapers and iron with a rag and cleaning fluid to keep them free from klister.

Klister also mates to boilerplate, the crunchy kind of slab or icecake snow (condition 5) caused by the freezing of thoroughly wet snows. This is "metamorphasized snow," so called because it is "radically changed." You can probably get by in "metamorphasized snow" with the purple klister, but a second type of klister (it is usually coded blue) called *skare klister* or "ice klister," will stay on better. Skare klister stays on even when the bottom of the ski is scraping ice constantly. It will give the ski a grip on ice without letting the ski itself ice up.

A Waxing Chart

There are at least 13 major wax companies with a complete line of waxes, with many gradations in each subdivision to help the cross country *racer* make up precious seconds over a race course. The *touring* skier is more concerned with practicality, thrift and simplicity. Therefore, he gets along with at most six: green, blue, and yellow sticks, two kinds of klister paste and a bar of paraffin. Add a cork and scraper and you have a wax kit.

Get to know one brand of wax well. Fix the color code in your mind. If you should, for instance, make a gross mistake in the color code and put on a klister-wax below freezing, you will get frozen wax, wax that will neither grip *nor* slide.

Here is the complete wax roster, three sticks, two tubes, and one bar.

Cold, loose, fine-grained snow = green or blue hard stickwax.

Clogging transition snow or cold "corn snow" = yellow klister stick-wax

Wet, mushy snow = wet snow klister tube

Boilerplate or ice cake = ice klister tube

Ice on the ski = paraffin bar.

Chart for Swix Waxes

Most manufacturers put out a waxing chart that shows the relationship of their range of waxes to the temperature, and moisture in the snow. The Swix chart is reproduced here: don't worry if you can't absorb it all at once. Use it as a reference, after you've had some experience.

The chart simply demonstrates that as snow ages and gets wetter and warmer, or re-freezes, you need softer wax. That's it.

New snow		Fine-flake old snow		Corn, crust, ice	
26° F and lower	green tin	12° F and lower	green tin	dry to moist (any temp.)	blue tube
26° F to 32° F	blue tin	12° F to 32° F	blue tin	wet snow (any temp.)	violet tube
at 32° F	violet tin	at 32° F	violet tin		
above 32° F moist (clogging) snow	yellow tin	above 32° F moist snow	red tin		
above 32° F wet snow	red tube	above 32° F wet snow	violet tube		

Trial and Error

Remember that the chart isn't foolproof. Only trial and error will really tell you the story.

Some practical hints:

—if you are going on a day-long tour, waxing right is very important. Try two different waxes on each of a pair of skis and see which seems best, and then re-wax the one that doesn't work as well.

—if the ski has started to backslide during a tour, putting on a dab of softer wax underfoot is a quick way to renew the ski's grip during the kick.

—if you are sure of the right wax, put on several thin coats before starting out, setting the skis out to cool between coats. This will last you much longer than one thick coat, and keep you from having to re-wax underway.

—remember the "people factor" in waxing: individual size and expertise. The beginning tour skier who has a weaker kick needs a softer wax than the experienced racer with a harder "kick," even in the same snow conditions. This goes double for kids. You may not be doing the child a favor by waxing his skis just the way you do yours. You may find he is much happier when you add a little "kicker" on the section of the ski under his bindings.

Further Mysteries of Waxing

We've so far implied that there is only one kind of snow out there at a time, but of course that isn't so. There are combinations of snow in a day just as there are combinations of weather in a day. For snow combinations, you can often use wax combinations.

Suppose it is a hot day and then the temperature drops below freezing and it snows lightly. There is an inch or less of loose, fine cold snow on top of icecake snow. What do you do?

First, put on ice klister and let it cool. Then, on top of the cool klister, crayon some hard wax and cork it.

Klister is technically softer than all other waxes, but it is so sticky it can act as a binder for harder waxes on top of it. Therefore, you can—in this case—use a softer substance underneath and coat a hard wax on top. The cold, fine snow on the surface will be in contact with the hard wax, but when the skis scrape ice, the ice will push through the layer of hard wax and contact the softer layer of klister.

Suppose you are going to climb a mountain—it has warm transition snow at the base and cool snow higher up.

Put on a coat of hard wax and then a coat of klister wax. The klister wax will wear off first, leaving the right wax for the cooler snow on the upper slopes. This will save re-waxing en-route. But this system will not work in reverse. Going down the mountain, a softer stick wax under a hard stick wax will erode off the ski quickly and your work will be wasted.

You can also mix waxes by putting different kinds of wax on different parts of the ski. For instance, you might coat the section directly underfoot with softer wax than is on the rest of the ski to meet a combination of warm snow under cool snow. The ski bites deeper underfoot than the tip or tail.

If you are out in dry snow and it starts to rain, your necessary rewaxing job should be paste klister. A torch will come in handy to dry the ski as well as warm the tube to make the klister spread easily. For a serious tourer, the butane or propane torch is a real tool.

A butane torch is much lighter than a propane torch, but butane must be warmed in the hands or next to the body in below freezing temperatures. Butane freezes to a mush and won't light. Propane torches are heavier but work well down to $-44°$.

Removing Wax

The tour is over. How do you remove wax?

Never remove old wax from your skis unless you are going to store them for at least a couple of days. Tomorrow's conditions may well fit today's wax job, and there's no sense waxing twice when once will do.

If, however, you have used klister and are going to put the skis in your bag or on your rack, take the klister off.

Take hard stick waxes off with a hand scraper. Rags soaked in gas or turpentine will finish the job, but be sure and do this

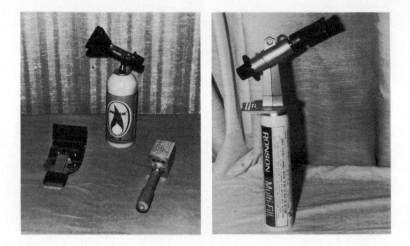

From left to right and top to bottom: The Primus torch runs on butane and has a flared flame guard to give wider flame. Waxing iron attachment on left fits over torch in place of flame guard and allows wax to be smoothed by both pressure and heat. Waxing iron on right is light and simple to manage. It burns solid fuel in pellets inside or can be heated by a torch from the outside. / The light Ronson torch burns butane. / The Bass wax kit has cork, scraper, three hard waxes, and a tube of klister ($5.50). / The Swix waxing "cork" is made of expanded styrofoam, which leaves fewer crumbs in the wax than real cork.

This combination scraper and cork has a holster into which scraper fits, keeping wax out of contact with surroundings.

outside. To remove klister heat it with a torch and scrape it off —or use turpentine or gas. Warning note: some of the commercial cleaning pastes when coated on klister and left to stand may also remove the tar. (Don't use cleaning pastes unless you know how they work. And on plastic-bottomed skis never use them unless the ski manufacturer specifies it.)

A commercial hand cleaner or plain vaseline will take blobs of klister off your hands. Don't use these to remove wax from *skis*. These substances can penetrate the ski bottoms and destroy the tar base you have so carefully put on.

Unfortunately wax can also get on your clothes. It seeps into fibers and weave of cloth, especially if warm. There are really only two ways to combat the problem: first scrape as much wax as possible off the clothing with a dull-bladed table knife. Then try either a dry cleaning solvent designed to dissolve wax, or the traditional remedy—place the cloth where the wax is embedded between two pieces of absorbent paper and press gently with a warm iron, replacing the paper until as much wax as possible has been melted out of the material.

Best of all, remember to wear a work apron when you use a klister or a torch the first few times.

Basic Wax Kit

Here's a check list of *all* you need for your first year of waxing:

Base tar
Tar brush
Hard green wax
Hard blue wax
Klister wax
Klister
Ice klister
Paraffin bar

Torch
Waxing iron
Waxing cork (expanded sytro-
     foam)
Scraper
Pocket thermometer
Hand cleaner (vaseline will
     do)

Carrying and storing the wax kit: klister is like a snake: it will seep out when it is warm. Carry klister tube wax in a cool outside pocket. Make sure the cap is on tight and it's in a plastic bag.

Over the summer, store all waxes in a cold place, wrapped in plastic bags, with a separate inside bag for each of the klister tubes.

The Future of Waxing

Tour-ski rental shops particularly need something better than waxing to speed the spread of touring. The problems of waxing and then cleaning a hundred pairs of skis with klister defies description. But in a few years, beginners may not have to wax at all. Ski manufacturers are working on ways to eliminate the need to wax. One proposed solution is a "fish scale," a raised surface type of base, with irregularities that allow the ski to move forward but retard the moving back. Another solution uses mohair, furlike strips under the foot, on the principle of mountaineering "skins," but much smaller than the traditional skins.

Nevertheless, waxing will never die out for the tourer who wants to make the most comfortable headway possible. Artificial bases and gripper mechanisms will only be able to approximate the action of a good wax job.

Wax will not die until touring does.

CHAPTER 4

Uphill and Downdale

The real excitement of touring comes when you get out into rolling country. Going up and down hill requires more expertise than touring on the flat—and considerably better waxing. To tour rolling country successfully, your wax really must hold well going up and slide well going down.

Not every stretch of snow-covered land is suitable for early up-and-downhill touring. You are immeasurably better off doing the exercises that follow on very tame terrain at first: the high green of the golf course, the twenty foot vertical rise at the edge of town, some already-cut logging trails in the woods, or bridle paths around the country club.

Touring is plagued with what has been called "the wilderness myth." The kind of terrain that brings out the best in touring is as scarce as good Alpine terrain. Organizations such as the Touring Council, and others listed in an appendix, keep tab on the good man-cultivated touring trails around the country. Touring schools, some of which are also listed in an appendix, mark and take care of good tour terrain. Tour terrain doesn't require much care, and can be constructed relatively cheaply.

When you start out touring in the countryside, avoid frozen conditions until you have had a chance to learn some of the downhill turns explained in this chapter. The downhill part of touring is often neglected in instruction books; consequently, a large number of people don't know that downhill tour skiing can be awfully fast. On hard crust, you *really* have to know what turn you are doing.

Alpine skiers who are confident they can handle the downhill touring may be in for a surprise. The touring ski is a very light contraption compared to the Alpine ski. My first experience touring steep downhills came after a good decade of rugged Alpine going. There exists an interesting series of photographs showing how I felt when, with pack on my back, I leaned forward into the normal Alpine downhill position, and found my heels coming up and my head going down.

This illustrates the primary difference between downhill in the two sports: ski touring bindings normally have no heel hold-downs. It is a pretty good idea to avoid heel hold-downs. They make touring considerably more risky. You can learn to make rapid descents without the heel hold-down.

The "telemark position" with one leg forward in a sort of supplicating position is a standard, extremely useful and necessary tactic in touring. The telemark running position enables the skier to negotiate steep terrain, bumps and hollows, without getting thrown forward. Bumps, drops and the like mean "go to telemark."

The sidestep and the herringbone demonstrated here are used almost automatically in Alpine skiing whenever the skier faces climbing a small hill. But these two are last resorts in tour skiing. It is worth all the care it takes to wax well just to avoid them. With good wax and sufficient practice, the tour skier can go *straight up* hills that would seem far too steep to negotiate that way.

Stott

Precise technique in downhill skiing makes downhill exciting.

Once tried and tested, the properly waxed well-versed tour skier can make great time in rolling country because he goes in a beeline uphill and rests all the way on the other side, sliding straight down.

Our first exercise is therefore the most important: the straight climb.

The straight climb. Pick a reasonably slack uphill for your first try at this. Modify the regular diagonal stride a bit, in order to keep your poles behind you always. That means the pole, instead of being inserted somewhere between the boot toe and ski tip, is inserted right *at* the boot (see the skier's far pole in the picture at right). On slack hills, the stride is a bit longer than the stride on the flat and there is no glide to speak of—only a long striding slide, at the end of which the skier presses his full weight on the ski to keep it glued in place (left, above). The second pole is inserted before the first pole is to be removed (second from right). Thus, there is very little chance to slip back. Any time there *is* a slip back, you have both poles behind you to catch the backward slide. (An unchecked backward slide can be very awkward indeed.)

If the wax is not holding well, it helps to slap the forward ski down into the slope instead of sliding it forward.

The steeper the hill, the shorter the stride.

Climbing also requires a more forward lean, and the knees are bent more. The weight is forward, so that the body goes over the forward-sliding foot.

The pole gives a harder push. Unless it is an awfully long uphill, the arms can take on much more strain than in flat terrain touring. However, it is a bad mistake to think you can pull yourself up by arm-power alone. The legs still do the greatest part—at least three-quarters of the work.

Never put the poles in ahead of the boots and try to climb up like an ape, hand over hand. Your arms won't make it, and you'll take so much weight off the skis that the wax won't hold. You'll lose both ways.

Once mastered, though, the uphill is a real showpiece for your talent. So, go to it.

Double poling for downhill. Believe it or not, once you start going downhill, you will often find you are going too slow, especially if the wax you've used is a little too soft. Soft wax is great for the ascent but sluggish on the descent. Double poling on slight downhills will add the thrust of two poles working together to give you a long glide.

On the flat, double poling relieves the muscular monotony of always doing things the same way.

To double pole, plunge both poles in at the end of one glide (third picture from left), and stride forward, both skis together, in a long glide, thrusting both poles out behind explosively (fourth from left). At the end of the glide you can either stick both poles in again without a stride, or you make one stride, and double pole—or two strides and double pole. Mix them up. Double poling increases your speed over a short distance but the arms soon tire. The arms' endurance is no match for that of the legs. Again, as in diagonal poling, concentrate on going *down* the track, not shifting weight from side to side.

Telemark running position. When your wax is working and your hill is steep enough, the telemark running position is your best friend. Here the skier approaches rough snow and a bump. He goes into the telemark, weathers the rough spot (third picture from left) and holds his position through it (fourth from left), making sure he has his balance before going back to a more erect, more feet-together position.

The telemark is executed by pushing either ski well forward, and kneeling by pushing the near knee down *toward* (not on) the rear ski, so that the weight is on the *toe* of the rear foot, and the *full length* of the forward foot. The skis are six to eight inches apart; thus, you have both fore and aft stability and side to side stability. You should use the telemark every time you feel insecure, or just practice it for fun.

Herringbone up the hill. The "herringbone" climbing step is for hills too steep for your present technique and wax. To herringbone, open the tips, pull the knees together toward the center line between the skis, putting the skis "on edge." Stamp the skis slightly "on edge" into the snow with firm alternate steps.

You must move the ski so the tail of one ski does not cross the tail of the other ski. It is an awkward, bowlegged gait, but it does get you uphill faster than the more elegant sidestep, the next exercise.

The pole work for the herringbone is just as important as in the straight climb. Put the pole in by your foot and push back. Never put the pole ahead of you. Put your hands on top of the pole handle as you push back and you'll get a better push.

The herringbone is a great safety device: if you try straight climbing and slip, simply spread the tips into the herringbone to stop yourself, and continue on up.

Sidestep up the hill. When all else fails, use the sidestep. You can climb a vertical wall with the sidestep. The sidestep is a simple two-step in which the uphill ski is stepped sideways a foot to two feet, and the lower ski brought up to it.

Both skis must be kept "on edge": both knees must be pushed uphill so that the edge of the ski bites into the snow at a sharp angle. It's no good trying to sidestep on a "flat ski," one that is flush with the snow, because the ski will slip sideways.

Plant the uphill pole at the same time you plant the uphill ski. This is one time you can "hang" on the pole. Put lots of down-pull on the uphill pole and push off hard on the downhill pole. You are not relying on the wax to hold you, but on the edge of the ski, and you can, therefore, put as much weight on the poles as seems necessary without causing the skis to slip.

Sidestepping straight up is the fastest and most strenuous way. On steeper hills, move forward with each sidestep and climb up slantwise, making what is called "the forward sidestep." If you run out of open hill in one direction, and come up against a woods, do a kick turn on the hill, making sure you face *down* the hill when you do it. Then start off slantwise in the other direction with a forward sidestep. On a steep hill, it is better to do a series of slants than try sidestepping straight up because you'll be able to progress without having to stop and rest. Keep the effort at a level you can sustain.

Step turn to a stop. Once you start skiing on steeper hills, you will want a simple way to change direction and, particularly, to slow down. The best way to slow down on a hill is to start going *across* instead of down the hill. The most obvious method is to make the same steps that you made for your skating turn on the flat. Pick up the ski in the direction you want to turn, and step the tip over that way, making sure you pivot it at the tail, so the skis don't cross at the tails. Put the ski down then and, almost immediately, pick up the other ski (picture farthest to the right) and bring it alongside the ski already moved. Three or four quick two-steps in a proper direction will slow you down considerably.

The skier in the top picture is going straight down the hill. This is known as skiing the "fall line." He picks up speed very quickly. The skier then makes a series of steps and is finally (bottom picture) running along the "traverse line," the line going straight across the hill. You will soon come to a stop running the traverse line as there is no gravity working along that line, only friction to slow you down.

In order to hold a traverse line, you do have to keep the ski on edge. Push your knees sideways a bit in the uphill direction so the uphill edge of the ski bites into the hill at a sharp angle.

Step turn to speed up. You may find yourself traveling quite slowly going down a hill on a slant. This means you are too close to the traverse line to get any benefit from gravity. Simply pick up the downhill ski, point the tip downhill, set it down (second picture from top) and then step the other ski down next to it (third from top). Repeat until you are in the fall line and going down quite fast, thank you. If this seems too fast, you can always step up toward the traverse line again.

Snowplow slow down. When you get to packed slopes, on a ski resort's trails for instance (there are lots of tour trails that utilize some of the regular downhill slopes at ski resorts), you will find that the step turn is not efficient enough to slow you down quickly. Use the snowplow instead. The skier above is running in the fall line (top picture). He splits the tails about as far apart as he can (middle picture), and keeps the tips together. He keeps skis fairly flat against the snow. This produces a braking force which the skier can hold to the bottom of the steep section.

The snowplow is the basic position for a series of downhill turns known to skiers for fifty years as "Arlberg" skiing, and, in fact, was used by Hannes Schneider to teach Austrian soldiers carrying heavy loads in Schneider's ski school in the Arlberg mountains. To give Nordic skiing its due, however, the Arlberg turn was *invented,* not in the Arlberg, but by Norwegian ski jumpers in the 1860's to turn to a stop after their jump. The first depiction of an Arlberg turn is in an 1888 Norweigan ski manual.

Until recently, Arlberg turns were the foundation of Alpine skiing, but Arlberg turns are being de-emphasized more and more in the new short ski or GLM teaching techniques now coming to the fore, that emphasize instead parallel skiing (skis side by side in the turn). Parallel is possible on tour skis as well, as the last part of this chapter shows.

Snowplow turn. The plow position can be used to change direction and, even more important, to steer the skis out of the fall line and into the traverse line where the skier will slow down. The principle of the snowplow turn is that both skis *want* to turn in opposite directions when in snowplow position, but the ski with the most weight on it has the most turning power. Therefore, lean harder on one ski than on the other and that ski will start to turn. Above, the skier is in a snowplow going down the fall line. As he leans onto the far ski, that ski goes into a very slow spin and gradually turns the skier toward the traverse line (bottom picture). The skier will slow down and, in fact, stop if he wants to hold that line. This is a great turn when you are carrying a pack because there is not much body movement involved. However, what movement there is has to be very pronounced. You have to lean on the outside ski of the turn; that ski quickly becomes the downhill ski (next to the last picture) so you are, in effect, leaning *down the hill.* This feels most unnatural; it takes quite a bit of practice before you get used to the feeling.

The trick to the snowplow turn is to lean hard on the downhill or outside ski, as well as to keep your weight well back on the heel of the boot, so that you get a good steering grip on the ski to permit the boot to hold the ski in the plow position.

The stem turn. The only difference between the snowplow and the stem turn is that before and after the stem turn, the skis are parallel (side by side). In the snowplow turn, the skis are always in the plow position, which is less restful. Here the skier, coming across on a traverse (upper picture), assumes the plow (or stem) position, and leans on the outside ski of the turn. In the stem, the outside ski is the uphill ski at first (third from top) and becomes the downhill ski later (fifth from top). You have to continue leaning on it all the time to push it through this turn. Your weight should be well on the heel of the outside boot so you can push that ski throughout the turn.

The stem turn can be fast or slow, depending on how much you put the skis on edge. The more the knees are pulled together toward the center line between the skis, the more the skis are on edge, and the more they will brake. Warning! If you put them too much on edge, you won't be able to start the turn at all. The outside ski, particularly, has to be kept flat enough to slip a little during the turn. If it won't slip, it won't turn.

The stem christie turn. This is a slipped turn, as opposed to the plow and stem turns, which are called "steered turns." (Christie means slipping or sliding. It is a contraction of "Christiania"—the name of Oslo before 1924.) The skier starts what looks like a stem turn, but instead of continuing to hold the tails apart, he plants the *inside* pole of the turn (third from right) and using this as a sort of vaulting pole, he lifts the inside ski off the snow and simultaneously vaults his weight quite suddenly and completely onto the *outside* ski of the turn. This dramatic move kicks the outside ski into a sort of sideways-forward skid. The inside, or lifted, ski is brought out, parallel to the skidding ski, and the skier finishes his turn skiing *parallel,* with both skis skidding side by side (third and fourth from right). This is a lovely way to finish a turn, far more elegant than the straddle of the snowplow/stem position.

The key to the christie is balancing *all* the weight on the single outside ski for the last part of the turn, and this takes a good bit of practice. If you cheat, and put part of the weight on the skidding inside ski, your skis will split from each other. A good way to practice the stem christie is to pick a slack hill and simply keep the inside ski lifted all the way through the last part of the turn. When you can christie, you are close to being able to do a parallel turn, the most exciting turn in skiing.

The parallel turn. The ultimate desire of all skiers is some form of pure parallel turn. In the parallel turn, the skis are always side by side. The stem position is replaced by a crouch with skis parallel (second from top) and a straight upward hop, triggered and helped by the inside pole (third from top). During this hop, both skis are turned sideways somewhat to the direction of travel. When the skier lands (fourth from top), his skis are already skidding sideways and forward. He simply rides the skis, with his weight well back on the boot heels (much more weight on the outside ski than on the inside ski) until the skis complete the skid and the turn is made.

The hard thing for most skiers to remember is that the skis have to skid sideways as well as forward to make the turn. This means they have to be set rather flat against the snow as the skier lands so the skis *will* skid. (They won't if they are too much on edge.) Most of the parallel turns that fail to come off do so because the skier edges too much when he comes down, or forgets to put nearly 100% of his weight on the outside ski of the turn—not an easy thing to do.

But to master the parallel turn is worthwhile, because with it you can ski in deeper snow. Tour skis give you a chance to get out to unsullied powder that no one else can reach: There are no lifts, and very few other *tour* skiers can ski deep powder. At this point, you are nearly at the pinnacle of fun in tour skiing.

Deep snow wedel. When the snow is really deep, you will need a form of parallel known as wedel (literally, "tailwagging"). This is a series of connected, cut-off parallel turns. Their utility in deep snow is that the turns are simply very snaky partial turns, one interrupting the other so that you are doing a wiggle a second, leaving a little snakelike track down the slope without getting turned into the traverse line. In deep deep snow, when you hit the traverse line it is dreadfully hard to get back into the fall line again to keep going. You stall. If you can wedel, however, you can ski the whole slope in one uninterrupted run.

In the top picture, the skier is turning slightly toward us, and in the second, he is turning away from us (the inside pole is away from us, planted in the snow). In the third from top, he is finishing the second turn, still turning slightly away, and beginning to plant the near pole to start his third turn. In the fourth picture from the top, he has planted his pole, gone by it for his third turn, and is now turning slightly toward us again. The fast pole work needed for wedel takes split-second timing and you won't learn to wedel from this book. But you can learn it from someone who can do it after you understand the principles explained here.

Steve Reischl at full speed downhill.

Many Alpine skiers who can already wedel will be able to wedel on tour skis after a few lessons. You have to keep your weight more firmly on the heels than on Alpine skis, and learn to sit back a bit more than in an Alpine binding, but as Rieschl shows here (and he's one of the best in the world at it) deep snow wedel on touring skis is a great way to go.

One warning: When you go into powder country, you go into avalanche country. Never go into avalanche slopes without *checking with the Ski Patrol* at the nearest resort, or with the nearest Forest Service officers to see if conditions are safe. You can die as quickly in an avalanche on a short powder slope a half mile from a lift as in the remotest valley in British Columbia.

Go in a party of four or more: If there's any kind of slide activity, get away from the slopes immediately. And always let somebody, preferably the Ski Patrol or the Forest Service, know where you are going and when you'll be back.

CHAPTER 5

The Outer Skier: Clothes and Equipment

Ski touring is generally an inexpensive sport. You *can* spend quite a bit of money for fancy clothes and for special features like bindings with optional heel tie-downs and unbreakable fiberglass skis. But it is not at all necessary.

The sport of touring emphasizes utility clothes. There is no status advantage and little practical advantage to appearing in expensive equipment. The average tour skier comes a lot closer to spending $100 than $400.

Furthermore, everyday winter outdoor clothes have much utility in ski touring. You do not continually ride a chair lift exposed to the wind; you maintain a reasonably even skin heat except when you stop and cool off. You are not exposed to the extremes of heat and cold that the Alpine skier is.

You don't need the heavy down parka; you only need a heavy sweater. You don't need expensive double-layer underwear that insulates; single-layer underwear will do. You don't *need* warm-up pants or knickers if you have a pair of heavy wool slacks already. In fact, if you want to tour in a pair of ordinary corduroy pants, with a couple of ordinary street sweaters, an ordinary dacron windbreaker, a standard shirt and ordinary wool mittens, you incur no social or technical disadvantage whatsoever. You can easily cut the $100 minimum price to well below $100 by using gear you already own.

The irreducible necessities are the skis, bindings, boots and poles. They should cost about $60 minimum. Any good touring store ought to be willing to outfit you for that price. (In Alpine gear, $60 is about the minimum price for a good pair of Alpine boots alone.)

Here's a list of typical equipment costs in high and low ranges.

Economy range		High range	High range feature
Skis	$ 25.00	$120.00	(unbreakable)
Bindings	6.00	40.00	(release heel)
Boots	25.00	40.00	(racing quality)
Poles	5.00	30.00	(unbreakable)
Sun glasses	5.00	25.00	(unbreakable)
Wax kit	5.00	15.00	(racing kit)
Mittens	5.00	20.00	(down and leather)
Knickers	15.00	25.00	(fashion label)
Hat	5.00	10.00	(fashion label)
Shell parka	15.00	35.00	(fashion label)
Long underwear	10.00	20.00	(fashion label)
T-shirt (turtleneck)	6.00	15.00	(fashion label)
Knapsack	5.00	30.00	(rigid frame)
Thick wool sweater or warm parka	15.00	50.00	(down parka)
Total:	$147.00	$475.00	

Clothing for Action

The essence of tour ski clothing is ease of walking movement. Don't buy clothing that hugs, binds or pulls, stretches or tears. You want loose-fitting, light clothes, woven for strength. The one exception to light clothing is the "rest garment," a heavy sweater or warm parka you carry in a sack to put on when you stop and sit.

Buy minimally to start with. If you have winter outdoor clothes now, make them do for at least the first tour. Maybe you won't *like* tour skiing. It is just possible you are an indoor addict (not probable: once on tour, nearly everyone likes it). So, look over your clothes closet first.

If you are already an Alpine skier, use your regular downhill outfit. Stretch pants, while they may be too tight for comfort on a longer trip (they keep pulling at your knees as you walk) are okay at first, since you won't—or shouldn't—be going all that far. If you have warm-up pants, wear them over warm light trousers; they will be more comfortable than stretch pants. If you have a warm parka but no shell parka, wear the parka without a sweater underneath. Leave the warm parka unzipped if you heat up. It may be a bit warm and heavy, but it will certainly do.

Remember this as you buy tour clothes: in touring, your motion will keep you far warmer than downhill skiing. Touring calls for continuous deep breathing and interior burning of oxygen, and that keeps you much warmer. Minute by minute you give off as much heat as a half dozen 100-watt bulbs. You burn enough oxygen in a day's touring to put out four million calories of heat energy (four thousand kilo-calories). A cross-country *racer* burns so much oxygen so fast he actually runs what in other circumstances would be an unhealthy fever, say about 102°. As a tourer, you won't run a fever, but, if you tour dressed *too* warmly, it will *feel* like a fever.

We assume in this part of the book that we are discussing a lunch hike, at most, a simple one or two hour outdoor session within reach of a warm shelter. However, if you do dress lightly compared to downhill clothing, you must still remember two things: when you stand still, in a class for instance, your warm "rest" garment will feel awfully good at temperatures around 10°; and if there is a stiff wind abroad, you will need the rest garment anyway. So, have it handy. If you don't have a pack,

Above: The classic touring ensemble: knickers, sweater and wool hat.

Below: Bonne Bell ski team wearing water-repellent "knicker bibbl-overs" by Liberty Bell.

bring the warm garment along and leave it on the snow near your class teaching area. And if you go off on a hike, carry the warm parka or sweater tied to your belt loops with a thong. This is handier, and cooler, than carrying it tied around your waist.

Staying Cool and Dry

Staying cool and dry is as big a problem if not bigger than staying warm. On a good day's tour, you may shed as much as two pints of water. Synthetic fabrics, unfortunately, won't carry off perspiration. Natural fibers will. Have at least one layer of natural cotton or fine wool next to your skin. Either will pick up skin moisture and transport it, like a wick, out where it can evaporate in the air, transmitting the cooling effect back to the skin. The hotter it is outside, the more you perspire and the more the wick action of natural fibers has to go to work to create a comfortable temperature inside your clothes.

If you block nature by enclosing your skin *completely* in synthetic fiber, waterproof cloth, or closely-woven windproof cloth, perspiration accumulates on your skin, any you will feel damp, sticky and cranky. When you stop, the accumulated perspiration will get very cold (in extreme cases, it will even freeze), and you will feel quite uncomfortable either moving or standing.

Waterproof garments are entirely *out*. They let no perspiration out at all. You'll feel clammy all the time.

Wind resistant knickers and long wool socks are the best below-the-waist combination when you tour at a reasonably good clip. There is enough windproof area in the pants to keep you warm if it blows, and enough perspiration-evaporating area in the socks to cool you as you get warm. The combination of knickers and socks is a good-looking, colorful, classic outfit, *and* one that actually works for your well-being.

Above the waist, proper aid to your natural cooling system is primary; you need a cotton underwear top under a light shirt or T-shirt, with a light wool sweater and a light windproof shell parka on top. (The parka definitely should have a hood with a drawstring for cool weather.)

The four layers above the waist provide all the options you need. If you feel too warm, take off the shell parka, and let the air stream through your sweater to carry off excess perspiration. If you are still too warm, take off the sweater underneath to enable your cotton T-shirt do the "wick work." The thinner the layer of natural fiber will have a faster and more efficient wicking action. Take off garments above the waist *as* you heat up. Don't let the perspiration rate overtake the rate at which the outer garments can evaporate it. You will get damp garments that you won't want to put on again if the air gets cold later on.

One of the best natural cooling fibers is your hair. A wool cap will allow the hair to draw perspiration away. Here again, if you get too warm, take off the hat and let the hair do it more efficiently by itself. In very cold situations, you may want a knit-hat-and-face-mask combination, the "Balaklava" hat.

The best bet for your feet are thin cotton athletic socks, white "gym socks," with wool socks on top. The cotton can wick perspiration away faster than wool. A two-layer sock system also

Carroll

Classic gear: wool pattern socks, light touring boots, toe clamp bindings, wood skis, heel plate, and bamboo poles.

absorbs some of the walking friction that otherwise may cause rub between a single sock and the skin.

Start your tour wardrobe with long cotton underwear, because it wicks well; if you need something warmer, try fine-spun wool, or wear a layer of wool underwear over the cotton (some people find wool next to the skin too scratchy). The classic long red underwear is a good top-layer underwear while pure nylon or dacron underwear prevents perspiration from reaching the next layer of clothes. Women may not like the idea, but a cotton bra and underpants are drier for touring than nylon ones. Give your natural cooling system a break.

In our modern commercial idiom, perspiration is something to be urgently concealed and suppressed. That idea leads to discomfort in touring. Leave your underarm deodorant on the shelf and take a nice healthy shower afterward. If all this seems elementary common sense, so much the better.

Staying Warm

On extremely cold days, you can carry insulated or quilted warm-up pants as well as a down jacket.

For medium cold days, a heavy sweater under the shell parka plus a pair of very light wind pants (shell warm-up pants) should strike the right balance.

Don't ever let a class situation awe you into standing stock still and freezing. If you are forced to stand around so long you do get chilly, jump up and down ten times, and then ten times more. You will warm up. If your upper body is cold, beat your arms quickly back and forth. Keep your parka zipper closed to the neck for warmth. (All zippers should have a thong attached for easy zippering with mittens on.)

The hands are a special problem: when they start to get cold, the blood supply in them is automatically turned almost off. Once the blood supply is cut way down, the hands will stay cold and painful unless you do something drastic. The best thing to do is warm your whole body up with a quick set of jumps-in-place, then crank the whole arm from the shoulder socket around in a complete circle, like a propeller, until the hand starts to warm up. The circular action drives blood back out into the fingers again by centrifugal force. But if you wear mittens rather than gloves, cold hands are less likely to happen at all.

Mittens and gloves of wool and windproof outer shells give you the most flexible response to heat and cold. A wool mitten with a windproof mitten cover is the safest; a wool glove with a mitten cover is warm enough at zero for some people. Leather-like Alpine gloves allow hands to sweat but don't remove the perspiration, so the hands get either sticky or cold. Those classic Norwegian wool mittens with the knit pattern are good looking and, like the classic knicker, are a very practical item. There are special ventilated racing gloves on the market but they are quite expensive.

The feet are another critical cooling point; your skis are extremely good insulation between the shoes and the snow, so be cautious about taking your skis off unless you have to. The problem of keeping feet warm is complicated by the fact that loose snow collects in the shoe opening and melts even in quite cold weather. This gives you a cooling system you don't need. And leaves you with wet feet, too.

The best preventative is a pair of snow gaiters or "powder cuffs" that fit over the boot and ankle. These cover the opening of the boot so snow can't collect and melt there.

If you find the shoe is not warm enough with a cuff in place there are "boot gloves," wool covers you pull over the whole boot. You can make an emergency boot glove out of a plain pair of extra socks with the toes ripped out so you can still keep your boot toe in the binding.

Factors in Natural Warmth

Your natural heating system, your blood circulation, can work well for you. Keep balancing the two: remove layers of natural fiber when you get warm; add layers of fiber plus windproof garments—and *move around,* which automatically increases blood circulation—when you get cold.

The question of heat-cold balance is actually quite delicate. Experienced skiers make frequent, and very fine, adjustments to it without thinking about it consciously and thus always appear comfortable even though they seem to have dressed quite by chance.

The more heat your body produces while you are on the move the lighter the clothes you can wear. Some tour skiers have to ski weighted down under heavy parkas because of low natural warmth while other skiers with more natural warmth happily wear light shell parkas and thin sweaters. Here are some of the factors involved in natural warmth:

If you take a good warm shower after a day's skiing, your body relaxes better: you will be warmer (and less tired, which is almost the same thing) the next day. You will feel colder the next day if you haven't had your eight hours, or whatever is your normal sleep time, the night before.

If you have over-imbibed and given your body a lot of extra work getting rid of the night's alcohol, you will be colder in the morning. Furthermore, alcohol will depress your heat-making capacity while underway.

Smoking constricts the blood vessels, automatically cutting down on warmth production. It is also harder to breathe deeply for a couple of hours after smoking. Shallow breathing and constricted blood vessels don't keep you warm.

The more physically tense you are, the colder you will be—therefore, an evening of fun (as opposed to over-indulgence) will keep you relaxed and warmer the next day.

Natural fat presents a problem in cooling off. An even layer of five pounds of body fat is much warmer than a whole layer of double woolen underwear. If you continually overheat and have trouble getting rid of your perspiration, a diet to drop five pounds will do wonders: It is easy to put on more clothes if you are cold, but hard to take off fat when you overheat. (See next chapter about jogging on skis.) On the other hand, other things being equal, a thin person needs more clothing.

Food as well as clothes relate to heat balance. A high protein, low bulk breakfast the day of your tour (eggs, cheese, fish, lean meat) will give you a good sustained source of blood sugar (energy) without leaving you uncomfortably stuffed.

The latest word on vitamins indicates that you may, under stress, need up to three times the "normal daily requirements." Take a couple of a one-a-day brand before touring.

A candy bar halfway through the day will not give you a fast pick-up; converting candy to energy takes two hours. For a fast pick-up use dextrose tablets, the quickest, easiest food to convert to energy: about 30 minutes.

Because you are perspiring, even if gently, you will tend to dry out and overheat, due to reduced perspiration, unless you drink water or juice during a full day's touring.

Touring Glasses and Goggles

A good pair of dark glasses, as much as proper clothing, is the most vital part of your personal comfort in touring. The amount of light that bounces off snow is two to four times the amount of light bouncing off normal landscapes. Most people don't know this, and they arrive without a pair of proper dark glasses and leave with a squint and a headache.

The most critical function of glasses is to remove ultra-violet light. After that, they should reduce the total amount of light. The best glasses do both without distorting the natural colors very much. There are several ways to go: half silvered glasses, for very severe light conditions, and any dark, high-quality "optical-grade" lenses.

Polaroid glasses do not work well in snow situations and in fact may be harmful—the explanation is quite technical, but true. Mountaineers' goggles are never polaroid. The polaroid process works well on water—but badly on snow.

Make sure that your sun glasses are non-polaroid, "optical-grade glass," or better "optical-grade plastic" (they won't shatter). Inexpensive sun glasses are always made of low-grade glass and give the illusion of cutting down light by cutting out all the bright colors reducing the landscape to sepia or some other weird color. They make your eyes open wide and let in too much ultra-violet light, which is bad for the eyes. Spend at least $5 for a pair of glasses—preferably $10. It is worth it to keep your eyes rested and your vision acute.

A good pair of glasses also improves the aesthetic value of your tour. After all, part of the reason you are out in the snow is to sightsee, not squint.

In a snow storm a pair of storm goggles are a godsend. You can see the trail, other people and trees without slowing to a stumbling walk. However, avoid yellow-tinted and orange-tinted glasses because these glasses tend to make you open your eyes too much to ultra-violet. Again, mountaineers never wear yellow-tinted glasses for good reason.

There are two good solutions to fog-inside-the-lenses which kills the usefulness of goggles. The first is a water-reducing film now coated on goggles such as Uvex. The second solution is a double lens goggle, with dead air in between. The only goggle with this feature is the Smith goggle. Both kinds will fit over normal sun glasses or prescription glasses. Buying other kinds of storm goggles is a waste of money.

Skis for Touring

Except when actually going downhill, the function of the tour ski is essentially different from that of the downhill ski. The tour ski functions as a foot, keeps you walking.

A foot made of pig iron would be a heavy load. So are heavy skis in touring. Alpine skis will weigh five to six pounds apiece; touring skis will weigh two pounds to three pounds apiece, about half of the weight of an Alpine ski.

The dynamics of tour skis prevent them from "holding" or tracking downhill as well as an Alpine ski, but the downhill part of the touring ski's job is least important.

Only in situations where the fragility of the lighter ski would make the expedition precarious, or where the downhill part of the tour is very important to the people involved and they want a regular downhill "feel" to their descent, should a heavy ski be used. But this latter is really "bushwhacking" and has little to do with true touring.

From left to right and top to bottom: Pattern hat in wool. / Norwegian snowflake pattern sock. / Touring skis and racing skis both have high tip, curved to lift tip above snow surface. / Traditional and new ski engineering side by side: left to right, Fischer Sprint Cross, a traditional, laminated, light touring ski made of hickory with lignostone edges ($27.00); Silent Spider, laminated hickory to a ring-racing ski with lignostone edges ($32.00); Europa 77 fiberglass sandwich with aluminum edges and plastic base, 2½ lbs each ($65.00); Europa, a metal sandwich, hollow wood core, plastic base ($36.00); Europa racing, fiberglass sandwich, hollow core plastic base, weighing 1½ lbs each ($80.00). / Cross section of new ski engineering: from left, Fischer Europa metal sandwich; Europa 77 fiberglass sandwich; Europa Racing hollow core fiberglass. / Comparison of light touring ski, left, with general touring ski, right, shows latter has greater breadth and is wider at tip.

Some stores and schools advise the beginner to try the sport on a regular pair of Alpine skis converted by means of a cable heel binding into a ski to use in touring. I disagree fundamentally. Not only do heavy, Alpine-weight skis give the beginner the wrong impression, they give him the wrong technique if he starts on them. Nothing can replace the light touring ski in learning; by touring ski we mean a ski weighing markedly less than five pounds.

What kind of touring skis?

There are three basic kinds. A fourth, the mountain ski, bridges the tour ski-Alpine ski categories.

The three basic kinds of touring skis are racing-touring, light touring, and general touring. Most touring skis today are made of the latest "miracle fiber"—wood.

The racing-touring ski is *very* light, about two pounds for the average (205 cm) length, and quite fragile. It is very close to an all-out racing ski, and is used by people who want to go fast over a prepared track or in very mild terrain. The racing-touring ski is a sports car model, with weight-saving a higher priority than strength. The bottom is usually birch, a lighter wood than hickory, perhaps with edges of hickory or Lignostone (beechwood compressed in resin). But the ski is really too fragile for most ordinary touring, in the way most sports car engines are too sensitive for ordinary road use.

The use of laminations of super-light woods make the racing-touring ski expensive. It is a narrow ski, almost as narrow as the special racing ski. For most tourers it is too specialized and too spooky in action.

Real Tour Skis

The real tour ski categories begin with the "light tour ski" weighing about 2–2½ pounds each, about 2″ wide underfoot, usually having a tough hickory sole. This gives the light touring ski plenty of strength and resilience for easy touring of the terrain. Since the light touring ski is almost as narrow as the racing-touring ski, it does need a fairly experienced tour skier to handle it well.

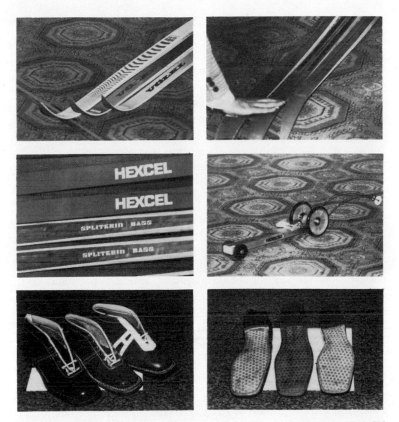

From left to right and top to bottom: Comparative constructions of Volkl skis: Loipe Sprint, wet-wrap fiberglass box with aluminum edge and foam core ($70.00); Vasa, wet wrap with P-tex and mohair bottom ($75.00); Racing, wet wrap with plastic bottom ($68.00). / Bottoms of Volkls shown in previous picture shows how mohair is placed on the Vasa model to eliminate traditional waxing: the mohair strips resist backward movement of skis, but allow relatively frictionless forward movement. / Splitkein Special is an old traditional brand with laminated hickory structure ($45.00), while Bass Hexcels are made with modern aluminum honeycomb ($87.00). / Like the other kinds of "summer skis" on the market, Nordic ($100) has a ratchet mechanism that keeps wheels from rolling back, and this makes it possible to practice touring on hard surfaces in summer. / From left, Fischer general touring boot ($30.50), light touring boot ($25.00), and racing boot ($32.00). / Soles of boots in previous picture show how (from left) general touring, light touring, and racing boots have increasingly lighter, less supportive construction.

The second true tour ski is the "general tour ski" which weighs something over three pounds, contains more and thicker hickory, and is somewhat wider and stronger. It is about 2¼" wide underfoot and therefore tends to ride higher in the snow, a particularly good feature for heavier skiers. This is the ski that most tourers use, and is in line with the tour ethic of utility. For the beginning tour skier, the advantages of light touring over general touring skis would be unnoticed, at least for the first few weeks; additionally, the downhill performance of the heavier ski is much steadier.

Never mind that the general tour ski would not make it on the international race circuit. It shares certain valuable characteristics with all Nordic skis. It is light compared with Alpine downhill skis. It is strong enough to take the terrain. It has a soft tip, for resilience in meeting snow, stumps, rocks and sudden upturns. Furthermore, it has the characteristic known as "forward spring." This means that the tail is stiff in proportion to the forebody of the ski. When the ski is set on the snow, and is pressed down, it will rebound up and *forward*, rather than straight up. This ski will actively help the tourer, giving its own little boost at each stride.

What length ski should you get? Length in touring skis is not quite the critical dimension it is in Alpine skiing, where every few centimeters registers a marked difference in performance and difficulty of manoeuver. Most tour ski manoeuvering is forward striding, and simple step turns for the beginner, perhaps coupled with a few straightforward stem turns on packed snow. If you are getting an inexpensive beginner's ski, you would do well to pick a ski about four inches taller than you are; this ski will be light and easy to handle. If you get hooked on the sport, you can buy a better-grade, longer ski later. A more experienced skier will want a ski about eight inches above his head. The proficient tour skier wants a pair ten to fifteen inches higher than he stands. The classic measurement method for the proficient tourer is to hold the arm straight up and let the ski tip come to the wrist, just below the heel of the hand.

However, if you are going to give touring a good two–three

weeks total time during the winter, you might well choose the proficient skier's length of ski, because by the end of your season, you ought to be reasonably proficient.

Mountain Touring

For mountain touring the *reliability* of the ski is critical. Losing a ski tip on a mountain can mean danger and, no doubt about it, the most vulnerable part of the ski is the tip.

One precaution for *every* tour skier, once he goes more than a mile from home, is to carry a "spare tip," a hollow aluminum or plastic tip that can fit over the broken stump and get the skier home. You can make an emergency spare out of a sock or mitten to keep a shredded tip from hanging up in the snow.

Even a supply of spare tips does not make most mountain ski tourers happy and comfortable. They want a heavier, stronger, somewhat wider ski, weighing about four and a quarter pounds apiece, with steel edges.

One solution is the general touring ski with a partial steel edge running under the main body of the ski. In mountain skiing, you will likely have to make some steep descents on hard snow (solid crust) and you need the bite of a metal edge.

Some mountain skiers go all the way and, for strength and performance, use a soft metal downhill-type ski such as the "Deep Powder" models of Alpine skis.

The emergence of fiberglass touring skis in the past couple of years has somewhat changed the picture outlined above. Fiberglass tour skis are more expensive, but they are nearly unbreakable. You could say that the emergence of the fiberglass touring ski eliminates the reason for the metal mountain touring ski: only the waxing problem of getting wax to hold on plastic bottoms need be licked. Fiberglass skis come with and without edges, and meet all the criteria for touring, from touring-racing to the ruggedest mountain skiing, depending on the model.

Before buying your skis, you should decide first of all how much you want to spend: you should spend $25 minimum to get good characteristics. Second, what kind of terrain are you going to be touring? If it's rugged ravines and unpacked trails, a wood general touring type is the least expensive and adequately reliable. Fiberglass is more expensive and stronger. For lighter going, in deeper snows, where you expect relatively smooth terrain, the light touring gives optimum performance and is less fatiguing.

Pick the actual skis by putting your own weight on them: set the skis on the floor of the ski shop and put a single thin sheet of paper under the arch of both skis. Put one foot on each ski so that the skis' camber is flattened, and the middle of each ski sinks to the floor. You should be able to pull the paper out. However, if you put three or four sheets of paper under, they should be pinned down by the skis. This is a way of ensuring that the skis are just stiff enough so that your weight flattens them to almost a straight line. This much camber and no more will give you the right "forward spring" for your weight and will spread the pressure evenly over the ski so your wax will wear evenly.

Too much camber and your ski will be so stiff it may throw you when you go over uneven terrain and wax will wear off on tip and rails. Too little camber and the ski will seem dead and unresponsive and wax will wear off under foot.

Touring Bindings

Touring bindings are divided into two categories: the ones that grab the very toe of the boot, the "toe clamp binding," and those that use a heel cable to force the boot into the toe piece.

Toe clamp bindings are far lighter. If you want a lightweight outfit, these bindings are great. However, you need more expertise to satisfactorily control a ski through a toe clamp binding—the connection is more subtle, less positive.

The heel cable binding, the "kandahar" type, is heavier, but makes it easier to balance on and to steer the ski. It confines the heel to a more limited arc than the toe clamp binding however, so you don't get as free-swinging a stride. On the other hand, cable bindings are more rugged, and last longer without breakage. They give a more positive control to the ski.

Probably the best approach to buying both skis and bindings is to contact a good touring school, if you are going to use one, and let them advise you. On your own, you probably are best off buying the general tour ski and cable bindings.

Clamp and heel cable bindings sometimes have a "heel tie-down" option. This means that you can tie your heel to the ski for downhill going. This makes downhill turning on packed snow much easier. However, it is possible to learn to ski downhill quite spectacularly, even through deep powder, without using a heel tie-down. And, when it comes to a fall, the free heel is very much safer than a tied-down heel. If you really want the downhill Alpine sensation because you are already a good Alpine skier, you might want to take the risk of a tie-down. But tour skiers are better off without it.

There's another heel appurtenance that every ski should have: a little rubber heel plate, or "pop-up" device, that will act like a de-icer boot on the wing of a plane. It is designed to depress and pop up again as the skier's heel hits at the end of each stride. This device keeps packed snow from building up under the repeated compression of the heel of the boot. It can save a lot of scraping-off time. The heel plate also helps steady the boot on the ski when going downhill and during the glide.

Touring Boots

Avoid the common error of trying to adapt hiking boots to touring: the soles are too stiff—a tour boot has a flexible sole. It is no good as a hiking boot. The opposite is true too. A hiking boot makes for hard touring.

The two kinds of proper touring boots are the "light" touring boot, which resembles a cross-country racing boot, and a somewhat heavier general touring boot, with higher sides, a rugged build, and metal edges forward on the welt of the boot to take the wear of a toe iron, the front part of the cable binding rig.

From left to right and top to bottom: Bass general touring boot ($25.00), compared to mountain touring boot ($35.00), shows the heftier construction of the mountain type. / Soles of general and mountain touring boots in previous picture show the greater thickness and width of mountain boot sole. / Rottefella ($6.95), a typical toe-clamp binding, extends to both sides of ski. Toe is held in place by short spikes protruding into holes drilled in sole. / Rottefella Phoenix toe clamp binding depends on the strength of the shoe to hold boot in line with the ski, leaves heel without any hindrance to upward movement. / Touring boot tends to extend slightly farther to the outside of the ski than the inside for proper weighting of the ski.

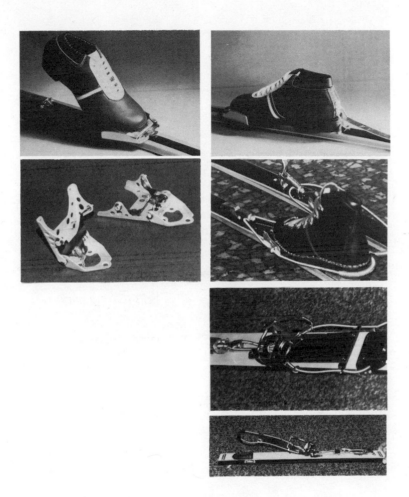

From left to right and top to bottom: The Eie toe clamp binding ($8.00) uses toe piece on boot to lock boot in place in toe clamp. / The Eie heel hold-down gives skiers more control in making downhill turns. / Still another form of binding takes some of the strain off the boot by providing pivoting toe plate. / Kandahar-type cable binding weighs quite a bit more than toe clamp type, but gives a greater ease of control over the ski. / The Silvretta mountain touring binding has a complete boot plate, which pivots up and down at the toe. Plate can be fastened rigidly to ski for downhill going.

The heavier boot is warmer, and will give you a steadier feel on the ski, especially at first. Those who are ambitious and have more time to perfect their technique the first season should try the light touring boot. You will save a half a pound of weight on each foot: a light touring boot weighs about a pound on each foot. The general touring boot is about a pound and a half.

When you buy bindings make sure you can fit your present boots to the bindings; if you buy boots, fit your bindings to them at the ski store. When buying boots be sure to wear the socks you will ski in; and make sure your heel can't move up and down easily inside the boot—the fit should be snug.

The Two Touring Outfits

The general touring outfit	*The light touring outfit*
general touring skis	light touring skis
cable bindings	toe clamp bindings
general touring boots	light touring boots

There are about three and three quarters pounds of difference between the two outfits; a mountain touring outfit will be another one to two pounds heavier in total; a regular Alpine outfit nine to ten pounds heavier than that.

Touring Poles

The classic touring pole is bamboo, and reasonably inexpensive. Like the light wood ski, bamboo poles do tend to break. Probably the best quality investment you can make in touring is in a pair of aluminum touring poles, which are light and break much less often. Nothing mars a tour more frequently than a busted pole.

The touring pole should be just long enough to tuck snugly under your armpit when you stand with the pole point stuck into the floor. This is considerably longer than the current mode for Alpine poles, but you do not use the Alpine pole as a vital part of your propulsion, as you do the tour pole.

From left to right and top to bottom: Two forms of cable binding: front-throw tightens cable (nearest binding); buckle-lever provides the necessary tension on the far cable binding. / Heel plates with moving rubber centers prevent snow buildup under heel of boots. / Powder cuff, or gaiter, keeps snow out of top of boots. / Warming sock can be drawn over boot in cold weather. / Four types of gloves, from left: Fischer alpine leather with synthetic insulation; leather cross-country racing glove with stretch insert; general touring glove with removable liner; general touring glove with permanent liner. / Adjustable pole strap on Allsop pole. Strap can be adjusted for the thickness of heavy mittens, tightened to fit snugly around thin racing gloves.

Heavy solid wood poles or heavy gauge metal poles are a drag in touring: make sure you get light bamboo or light aluminum. They have the proper "spring" to propel you and the right weight to be carried effortlessly all day.

Get poles that have an adjustable-length hand strap. You may want to use heavy mittens one day, light gloves the next, so the straps should tighten or loosen to fit closely but without "choking" the wrist.

The Tour Pack

You don't need an expensive pack unless you are contemplating a daylong trip involving two or more meals. A simple sturdy cloth bag with shoulder straps will do. You should buy one early on. It should have a flap that buckles down snugly over the top and several accessible side pockets. You can carry your rest garment in this bag, a couple of oranges as a thirst quencher, and a candy bar. These things come in handy even in a class situation.

An array of poles: from left, Garcia plastic-coated bamboo pole with shaped handle; bamboo with classic cork handle; fiberglass pole with cork handle; junior bamboo pole with pistol grip.

If you're going afield, add a plastic or aluminum spare ski tip and a light rain jacket, which is useful for sitting on. And very useful if it should rain.

Another useful item to carry is "Moleskin" or alternatively, big square bandaids in case your boot chafes. If you apply the padding over the sore spot on the foot in time, you will ski tomorrow. If not, it could be very doubtful. A blister is as painful as a bee sting—all the time.

Lastly, carry a spare pole basket if you can install one on your present poles, and a thong to replace a pole strap, should one break.

Care of Equipment

Resist the temptation to waterproof your boots. They will then lose their ability to breathe, i.e., evaporate moisture through the leather. Wax or non-clogging polish, yes. Waterproofing grease, no.

If your boots are very wet after your tour, stuff some newspaper in them and let them dry out by absorption. Do not put leather boots over a hot radiator or hot air grill; they'll crack and split.

To store skis for the summer, give them a regulation tar base treatment first, to keep them from absorbing moisture. Then lean them, tips down, against an inside wall to dry. This allows moisture to drip off without collecting under the butt end where the water will warp the ski. If you have very old skis, you block them up when storing, with tips and tails tied together and just enough wood blocks in between them to keep the camber as is. However, new skis are cambered to stay in shape without blocking.

You can use your skis in November without treatment if you treat them properly when you store them in April. The important treatment comes *before* storage. After that, in season, just tar as the base wears down. But *untarred* skis stored all summer may dry out and then absorb moisture and so come unglued.

In the old days, when all skis were solid wood (not laminated), they used to be blocked for the summer. The absence of glued layers inside caused solid skis to dry out during storage. In order to restore their resilience, these skis had to be left outdoors to absorb moisture. Today this procedure applies only to a very limited number of cheap solid skis sold. (If your skis are in the $15 range, you should check to see which way is the right one.)

If a bamboo pole cracks, strengthen it with plastic tape.

CHAPTER 6

Jogging on Skis to Lose Weight and Improve Your Condition

If Darwin was right, human beings descended from forms of life most efficient and aggressive. Man first dominated some of the animals because he was tougher. (The aboriginal could outrun deer by outlasting it over a day or so of running.) He dominated other animals by brain power. He had enormous reserve energy which went into outthinking the sabertooth and wooly mammoth.

The emergence of man as the dominant being on this planet depended on his extremely efficient production of energy: energy for endurance, speed, and—what takes quite as much energy as the rest of his body—his brain activity. Leaving brain activity aside for the moment, to build a machine that could duplicate some of man's cruder physical activities, such as lifting or running, as efficiently as the human body, is still a task beyond our capability. A man-like physical performance by a machine calls for an enormously potent and complex energy source. Man himself can derive energy for his physical activities from a few short daily rations of meat, cereal, a fruit or two and some vegetables. Science can't duplicate that, yet.

The Efficiency of Man

We are trying to make two points here. First: man can expend more physical energy over a longer period of time than most land animals and still have reserve thinking energy left over. Second: he derives this energy, day after day, from a small quantity of fairly low-energy stuff, known as food.

Man doesn't need exotic fuels, hot current or even a hot fire. He needs only a lukewarm body temperature of 98.6° F. He is a very efficient sort of construction, extremely sophisticated in energy-extracting processes: none of us can exercise this sophisticated body of ours into starvation. The body can easily respond by consuming a little more food to make up the additional energy loss. Therefore, it is possible to jog, run, tour, whatever, and still *gain* weight. The very first reaction of the body to increased exercise is an increased appetite. Food tastes just great.

But if you are serious about losing weight, then jogging on skis—which is simply sliding and gliding on skis over distance courses without undue regard for form or speed—can be a good way of going about it. If you tour on skis at a mild rate, you can burn up two to four hundred calories of energy an hour, a thousand in three hours. Theoretically, that would be enough to take off about two or three pounds a week, provided you toured for three hours every day and kept the same level of eating.

The body reacts to unfamiliar exercise by assuming that there's an oncoming emergency which may last God knows how many days. Appetite and food consumption zoom almost compulsively. The body starts to store up energy in the form of fat at a great rate. After a couple of days, maybe as much as a week, the body seems to relax its warning system a little, and your appetite goes down even though your exercise continues. *Then* you begin to lose weight.

Massie

The author jogging across Brooklyn Bridge toward Manhattan after a New York City blizzard.

The Secrets of Losing Weight

The first secret of losing weight by touring is to be patient.

The second is gaining the motivation to tour on any given day for a rather long time period. This means you have to get good enough at touring to learn to love it. It's no good trying to lose weight quickly by driving yourself to tour, so that it becomes drudgery. You will quickly give up touring if that is the case. You have to *become* a tourer, not try to *conquer* touring. This means you have to get into good enough condition to sustain moderate tours for a given period of time on any particular day.

Let's see why it is necessary to tour over a longer period, at least forty minutes or so, to lose weight.

To lose weight by exercising, you have to burn up accumulated fat. But the body has several ways of converting food to energy. The first is from existing blood sugar. Blood sugar will fuel your exercise for the first minutes of any exercise period. This won't lose you any weight because your body will replace blood sugar on a priority basis at the very next meal. After you use up your blood sugar (the level drops) you start drawing on your fat reserves—which is what you want. Only if you keep on going will your body reduce its stored fat.

Intermittent-activity sports, such as tennis, baseball, golf, sailing and downhill skiing are not very efficient weight-subtractors. There's probably not forty minutes of active running in two or three hours of average tennis, for instance. You could play tennis all afternoon without losing an ounce of fat; you merely lower temporarily your blood sugar level.

You have to be able to sustain an "aerobically demanding" activity in order to lose weight by exercising. Aerobically demanding means an activity that causes you to burn oxygen steadily to provide energy at a good rate over a sustained period of time.

The New Idea: Aerobics

Aerobics has become the newest way of approaching diet/exercise: the theory of aerobics is to measure a person's overall health in terms of an "aerobic level" that he can sustain. A common measure of aerobic level is the distance you can run in twelve minutes. If you are in good shape, you can run a mile and a half or more; in very good shape, you can do a mile and three quarters, or better.

The aerobically demanding sport consumes more than the normal intake of oxygen per minute over a period of more than ten minutes. Ski touring is aerobic, *par excellence*. If you want to lose weight touring, it is no good sprinting a hundred yards at twenty miles an hour on skis. But touring for an hour, at three or four miles an hour, will do you quite a bit of good.

Ski touring is aerobically demanding because you are using both arms and legs at the same time. (In plain jogging you are using arms almost not at all.) You don't need to move like a gazelle to lose weight ski touring. You can go, say, half as fast as you move in running and still get the same weight loss.

How much weight can you lose?

This depends on 1) keeping your food intake steady at your previous level, 2) how much touring per day you undertake, and 3) how big you are to start with.

Below is a theoretical weight-loss table for a 180-pound man and a 130-pound man. (Don't take this too literally—it's only an approximation.)

Hours of moderate touring	Weight loss at 130 pounds (in pounds)	Weight loss at 180 pounds (in pounds)
1	⅛	⅙
2	¼	⅓
3	⅜	½
4	½	⅔
5	⅝	⅚
6	⅔	1

This table shows two things. First, the thinner you are the more you have to work to lose weight. (Actually, this is a good thing because it means you won't fade away to a skeleton through touring.) Second, even in an aerobically demanding sport, you have to be patient. The human body runs far on very little weight loss.

(What the chart above refers to is, of course, permanent weight loss. By the time you've toured six hours you've perspired two pints of water, and lost two pounds of water, but the body replaces water on a high priority, so that loss is quite temporary.)

For those of us who are already thin enough (the lucky ones) these figures can be translated back into extra food we can eat without gaining weight. Since a pound of weight equals roughly 3600 calories, a 180-pound person can enjoy the following extras without gaining an ounce:

Hours of moderate touring	Food equivalent	Calories
1	Pork chop	300
2	Lamb chop and cheesecake	600
3	Celery soup, creamed chicken and cherry pie	1200

This means you can tour and eat very well, provided you are *not* trying to lose weight. This is a rewarding facet of tour skiing.

Touring: A Test of Fitness

Moderate touring speeds are approximately 50% faster than jogging speeds off skis. This is due to the extra thrust supplied by the arms and the glide of the skis. By aerobic standards, you are in good shape if you can go 1½–2 miles in twelve minutes of touring, assuming gently rolling terrain.

But 80% of the people in the United States don't qualify as being in good shape, by any test of aerobic level. The aerobic goal is to bring you up to this level of performance. The goal of weight-loss is less important than your ability to give a sustained aerobic performance. If you're overweight but can make it through two and one-half miles in twelve minutes touring, you are very likely in reasonably good health; if you are sliver-thin, but unable to give a sustained aerobic performance, you are not in such good shape.

Recent health studies of Americans show that until now, we've missed the point: We've emphasized muscle, and quick speed, weight lifting, and intermittent activity sports like tennis, bowling, golf, while the real health problems crop up around the lack of ability to do something *moderately taxing over a reasonably long period of time.*

We've been mesmerized by natural athletes with fast hands and miracle muscle-builders when we should have been studying the long-distance runner.

The Most Important System

Good functioning of the heart-lung system, is much more vital to life than speed afoot or stationary lifting power. Push-ups and downhill skiing can be done quite successfully by people who are not really in very good health. Our society encourages us to believe that there are natural athletes who are super healthy as opposed to the rest of us, who are not. But the most recent studies show the natural athlete who ceases activity at thirty gets degenerative diseases in his forties. The continuous practice of activity is necessary to health. You can't bank on past activity. A week in a hospital bed or a couple of days weightless in space is enough to cause serious degeneration of muscle tissue even in very healthy people.

A very reliable indicator, the best indicator, in fact, of your physical health, is your capacity to breathe oxygen in sustained quantity, and burn it over a sustained period of activity. That sounds simple, and it is. It doesn't require lightning hands, and superb broken field running but it does require the ability to take a lungful of air without coughing and a good set of blood vessels to carry off the oxygen intake and bring back the waste carbon dioxide. Only steady, patient, continuing aerobic activity can create and preserve that kind of capacity. You may have stick-thin legs, scrawny arms and a scarecrow neck, and still be in fine physical shape, because you continually, throughout your life, do some form of moderate but sustained aerobic exercise nearly every day: swimming, jogging, touring on skis, cycling— even fast walking, cutting sugar cane, hay-pitching, or modern dance.

Of all of these, ski touring is the most effective. It accounts for much of that famous Scandinavian health. The highest oxygen consumption of any group of athletes during performance is that of the international class cross-country racers who breathe eighty milliliters of oxygen per minute, about twenty times the amount you breathe at rest.

You can re-activate—luckily—aerobic capacity once it has declined, and get back the energy and sparkle that go with it. Even daily office work demands oxygen; if we can deliver it easily, we'll leave the office feeling more like dancing and less like collapsing in front of the television set.

The Aerobic Level

Why is reserve oxygen-consuming capacity (aerobic level) so important? It is at once a measure and a cause of the heart capacity and the condition of the arterial system. A good strong heart and good clear arteries, free from fat deposits, are the best insurance against heart attacks, and heart attacks are now the number one adult health problem in the United States.

The age at which coronary attacks occur frequently has been going down and down as our age of "retirement" from sustained aerobic activity has gone down and down. Today, one out of four or five eighteen-year-old Army recruits shows signs of aging arteries. They have lost full capacity and resilience. The heart and arteries of such people have almost never been taxed by activities beyond walking, standing, and sitting, since they were twelve. It's perfectly possible in the twentieth century for teenagers to live like hens in mesh cages. All they have to do is get to school every day. The hen is sacrificed early and tender: this is becoming the fate of the civilized coronary system, too.

What happens when you take up aerobic conditioning?

For one thing, you will breathe in more air. The truth is, the average man doesn't use much of his interior lung area for breathing. He has oxygen-receiving sacs in there that haven't seen oxygen for years. As a result, his capacity to breathe more air for increased activity is continually decreasing. Excess lung capacity over normal is a pretty direct measure of health. As excess capacity decreases, so does life expectancy. If you can't breathe enough extra air to go upstairs without panting, your physical activity decreases, your muscles get slacker—it's all downhill from there.

Aerobic conditioning increases the supply of blood to the muscles. Whole small fans of new blood vessels form: the result will be less daily fatigue, more reserve power. The amount of oxygen carried to the muscles and tissues is directly related to the waste products carry-off rate (fatigue-resistance) and to the ability to keep up a reasonable level of moderate activity, such as jogging, or touring.

Even more important, aerobic activity increases your body's ability to metabolize (break down and utilize) fats, instead of leaving them to deposit in your arteries and narrow the diameter and harden the walls—all conditions leading to coronary attack.

Aerobic conditioning also *rests* your heart. The heart will beat faster when you tour, for sure, but the aerobically conditioned heart tends to get somewhat stronger; it beats less often when at rest. You can save an awful lot of heart beats per year, save them for later, in effect, by putting your heart into good condition through aerobic activity.

Without getting too preachy, ski touring can be good for your insides, as well as give you a better looking outside. You can get back some of the fantastic potential that, when actualized, makes the human being the most durable and dominant physical entity on the planet.

Systematic Weight Loss

If you decide to make a serious attempt to gain aerobic benefits from touring, as opposed to just learning to tour intermittently, then you should proceed systematically.

You should, if you are over thirty, first get your family doctor to okay the project. He may want to check your heart occasionally, and that is only prudent. If you should have a technical heart problem, such as a not-quite-right-valve or some other non-aerobic weakness, then pushing forward with a jogging program, on skis or off, might not be too productive, and might even be damaging.

Don't worry, however, about getting the so-called "athlete's heart" or "enlarged heart." You can't damage a good heart by undertaking fairly energetic exercise. An enlarged heart is a heart that has already had to cope with some malfunction. You don't get it through exercise.

A word of caution: Don't try to attain the ranks of the aerobically fit in one wild swoop. If you exhaust yourself the first day trying to make one and one-half miles in twelve minutes, you're missing the point. What you are aiming for is to do it *easily*. Don't push or punish your body. Normally, it takes a couple of months of workouts before you make a very noticeable improvement. It takes that long for "vascularization" (new or improved blood pathways) to be effected, and for the heart and other tissues to get used to the new regime. The body is superbly able to adapt to increased demands. That is true right through old age. But you must let it adapt at its own rate and not try to force an overnight improvement.

If you are also planning a weight loss, remember that a five pound weight loss is a big body change. You need less blood for the same purposes, and your internal chemistry needs to adjust. Be happy with a gradual, permanent loss. Don't be discouraged when you lose three pounds by dinner and have gained back two by breakfast. This is only recouping your water loss.

Distance and Diet

The best touring track is a natural one. If you can go through varied country, woods and fields with some uphill and some downhill, you'll enjoy it more and stick to your everyday schedule more effortlessly. If you have to make a track in a suburban environment, try to make your run go past some point of interest, a park, a good-looking church, or whatever. Try to avoid the "lap psychology" in which you run around and around a sterile field.

The distance you run is less important than doing the distance every day and increasing the distance gradually. Tour for at least ten minutes. Then try to lengthen the time to eleven, to twelve, and finally, if you persist, you'll find yourself looking forward to going longer stretches. This is a sure sign of better aerobic condition.

Cool off slowly after you tour. An ice-cold changing room may lower your resistance to infectious diseases.

There has been so much said about diet, it's hard to say more. In the final analysis, if you take vitamins and eat balanced meals (lean meat and fish, raw fruit, green vegetables, go easy on bread, butter and fat and super-easy on sugar) your total quantity of intake is as important as anything else. Don't eat seconds. Eat a modest first. You will lose weight. Your diet should not leave you feeling tired and unwilling to get on skis or something is wrong with it.

A systematic approach, with planned menus, makes a big difference, not because there is any magic in planning, *per se,* but because you will know what you are doing, and you can vary the diet to see what the effect is. Most over-eating is done under the cloak of under-planning.

Exercise for Touring

A funny thing will happen on your way to aerobic touring. You'll get as strong as you need to be. Why add muscles you don't need, which will take sterile exercising to maintain?

However, if you are twenty-five or over, you may find stretching exercises, as opposed to strength exercises, help you relax while touring and feel less stiff afterwards. Work on being able to touch the floor. Stretch your arms overhead, do low back bends, and be able to sit on the floor and touch the toes with your legs stretched straight out in front of you.

One special stretching exercise will help: You probably need to get used to expanding your chest unless you have been doing regular aerobic activity. Lie on your back and fill your lungs to bursting; then keep the lungs expanded by taking very shallow breaths, expelling air in little pants by quickly drawing in and then relaxing the stomach muscles. Repeat the drawing-in twice a second. Hold your chest high under your chin as long as you can. Then let the air all out and repeat. This exercise will really help open up the area inside the lung to capture more oxygen.

It is a potent exercise, so do it very gently at first and for only ten or fifteen seconds. The increased oxygen may make you a little dizzy at first. Stop as soon as you get a slightly dizzy feeling.

Take a hot bath or shower after each day's tour: this will relax you more than any other single thing you undertake, outside of the tour itself. Above all, try to do your touring so you enjoy it. You want to make touring pleasure, not pain.

CHAPTER 7

The Lunch Hike and Tour Games

The lunch hike, or day tour, is a modest, satisfying way of extending your touring, and a good number of long lunch hikes will give you a fine start on the experience necessary for an overnight ski hike.

With some friends, I went on a lunch hike near Aspen that remains one of my memorable days. There is no better way to describe the rewards of day touring than to tell that story.

An Aspen Lunch Hike

We met in front of the Snowmass Sports Shop in the little village square—six people bent on getting away from it all into the woods to the east of the Snowmass lifts. We rented our little touring skis and soft boots, and away we went up across the beginner's slope in that soft little shuffle-and-glide that shows you know at least something about touring. Lars Larsen, cabinet-maker, hunter, guide, ski instructor and touring expert, with a cute little Swiss hat over his rapidly–mooning forehead, slid off in the lead. Pretty soon, he had us as out-of-the-way as if we'd been dropped into the back country by parachute.

The woods around Aspen are just incredibly great. Even where the aspen and spruce stand thick, there is always a way through them. The mountain is spotted with glades; you ski from one to the other. The Alpine skiers on this particular day were fighting a dull light which rendered the downhill slopes lethal at speed (you couldn't see a bump before you hit it). They had to bear a white stinging of light powder snow streaking for the ground in arrowlike lines. We were in the woods, skiing along at touring's "sweet speed." For us the snow flakes, respectful of the forest, slowed down to a lilting drift, settling like leaves to the forest floor. We skied single file.

The essence of touring is a companionable kind of slow Indian prayer dance for good crops. You all step forward together —everyone picks up the talk. No good touring group should get going so fast that people get out of breath. Talking is part of it. Touring is for people.

With Lars Larsen leading we trekked through glades, wound between spruces, mostly climbing, with our ski wax keeping the skis from slipping backward, yet sliding easily when we moved the ski forward. Thus, we could go up fairly steep hills with skis pointed straight up, leaning the weight on the sliding ski, making the smooth even movements that keep the skis from breaking loose from the critical friction that holds them. We climbed almost fly-like, on the upward sloping terrain.

The snow silted down through the trees, the branches bore their gift of ermine, bowing under the obligation; the skis made soft sounds, as they sank and compacted snow with each stride.

We realized we had climbed, in two and a half leisurely hours, the same distance that you ride in twenty minutes on the Snow-mass lifts; we enjoyed the terrain with corresponding intensity, cherishing it bit by bit.

When we got to a lean-to we stamped around, collected some dry spruce branches, threw them on a platform of larger branches, and set fire to it, grilling meat on a screen which, rolled up, is carried in Lars Larsen's pack, and can also be used for splinting legs. We made tea-with-brown-sugar and ate peeled oranges, thoughtfully leaving the bright rind on the snow for the birds, the Camp Robbers, who were dancing around in the branches in a minuet of ecstasy, waiting for the feast to begin when we, the intruders, left.

We started down. Sovereignty belonged to nature, not us. We were moving down, circling through the groves, seeking passage where the glades would admit us, snaking between the sinewy aspen; ghosts drifting down, a silence of skiers, the only sound attesting to our presence the sibilance of the skis cutting the crystal serenity of snow. End of story.

Successful Day Tours

We've expanded here at the beginning of this chapter on the joys and the adventure of touring. Touring often takes place quite a distance from civilization. We are city dwellers, not used to thinking in terms of self-help—no garage, no phone, no warm-room immediately available.

Day tours require five times the planning needed for a two-hour tour. It's so easy for any tour to go wrong. The success of day trips depends on a firm foundation of good thinking.

Day-long touring, as opposed to two-hour skiing (you find out), means you can run into a cold weather test. Cold is not a problem as long as you keep moving, but once you go immobile for your lunch break, you have to keep yourself warm with some sort of good body insulation, to substitute for activity-heat. It's a whole different ball game. You must have "rest garments" for everybody—preferably down parkas.

Day tourers must have enough touring technique to hold a straight line and make some step turns. Don't try to learn to tour on a tour.

Above: Land cruiser makes a fine place to begin and finish a lunch hike.

Below: Climbing into the Colorado mountains starts a day's outing.

The tourers must either know the whole neighborhood they are touring in, so that they can find the way out no matter where they are; or have scouted the trail ahead of time before committing a group; or, if the terrain is unknown, tour in just so far and backtrack. You cannot estimate tour time by map miles. Slippery conditions, deep snow, windfalls, lots of fences— all may slow your progress to less than one mile an hour.

It's no fun if everyone goes home tired, cold and hungry, or the group gets lost or runs way over estimated time, and has to worry about when in the world they *are* going to get back. Late return is perhaps the most common failing of group tours.

In a large group, the leader should know the group's capabilities so he can estimate their time over *known conditions*. If he doesn't know the group, he should estimate speed at one mile per hour. No fooling. He must *not* let anyone get over-tired. If anyone shows signs of fatigue, he either rests the whole group or sends the tired skier back with a member of the group to accompany him. In any event, the group must proceed at the natural speed of the slowest skier. Do not force anyone to press.

The leader should carry a topographical or small scale map and flashlight. (A map in the dark is no good without one.) You cannot assume, even though you know the neighborhood well, that you won't make a wrong turn.

Have some kind of food break, three times a day at least— once in mid-morning, a lunch break, and once in the afternoon —if you are staying out all day. You will be well-rewarded by the simple expedient of carrying enough oranges for everybody at mid-morning, a simple sandwich or hamburger for lunch (see Chapter Ten on tour cooking), and a candy bar or hot chocolate for mid-afternoon, when a sugar-food will keep people from becoming tired a bit later.

Fire and Warm Food

One of the best ways to treat people well is to make at least one of the food breaks a hot food break: this means building a fire. For fuel, use the dry twigs you can break off. Carry a small axe or heavy knife and cut little slices into small branches to make them burn. If the woods are protected, or you are touring where trees are sparse, bring one of the small butane or propane stoves that only weigh a pound or so. The morale and nutritive aspects of a fire are great. They are probably not really needed on a day trip, but on overnights, they are a necessity.

Carry matches (plenty of them) and some crumpled paper to start a fire. Carry matches in a waterproof case, and paper in a plastic bag, to keep them dry. Moisture has a way of rising from the snow and infiltrating everything. In a good wind, a simple match may not do the lighting job very well or at all. Build the fire under the screen you carry rolled up in your pack. This makes a fine grill. Once the fuel is under the screen, quickly light the rolled-up paper to start the fire. Cigarette lighters are fine, if they work. But don't depend on them. Flints wear away and lighter fluid dries up. Butane lighters may not work in the cold very well.

Stott

Open country is its own reward in touring.

Be Ready for the Problems

Carry necessary emergency gear and know-how.

Your "emergencies" will likely be the kind we've anticipated in the process of learning to tour: sticking or slippery skis, a chafed heel, a broken ski tip, a lost pole basket, a broken hand-strap, a scratch, a loose or malfunctioning binding, cold hands and cold feet, tiredness, headache, overheating, upset stomach, general chill, sunburn, windburn, eye-ache, sprained ankle.

Some of these problems call for a process, others for gear.

Sticky or slippery skis: minimum wax kit

Broken ski tip: spare aluminium or plastic slipover tip

Chafed heel: moleskin, or a big bandaid, mercurochrome

Scratch: mercurochrome, merthiolate, small bandaid

Loose or broken binding: a minimum tool kit containing plastic tape, a roll of stout cord, a short piece of copper wire, pliers, screwdriver, spare screws, knife and awl

Cold hands: spare mittens in case mittens are wet; also swing the arm around in a circle from the socket, until the hand warms up

Cold feet: a spare set of cotton stretch socks in case the socks are wet; an old pair of wool socks with toes cut out to slip over the touring boot for warmth if wetness is not the problem

Tiredness: dextrose pills

Headache: aspirin

Overheating: take off some outer clothes

Chill: put on a rest garment or wind pant shell

Sunburn, windburn: suntan oil which doesn't evaporate; for extreme cases, sunscreen cream.

Eye-ache: a spare set of good sunglasses

Serious Problems

A sprained ankle can be a hairline fracture. It is *not* a good idea for anyone to "walk it off." If they have a sprain and it continues to hurt, it may be a break.

Before we discuss breaks, we should have a word about the incidence of touring injury. It is very low. When 100,000 people tour, as often happens on Easter Day in Norway, it is rare to have more than one or two broken legs or serious sprains reported. Often none are. Don't confuse the injury incidence of touring with the injury incidence of Alpine skiing: when 100,000 Alpine skiers are out for a day, you will have an average of fifty broken limbs or bad sprains. This seems excessive, and it is.

Back to our injured tour skier: you should have some sort of water-repellent tarpaulin available. Put the injured person on this. Wrap him in spare rest garments, and cool the injured part with snow if it looks like a sprain. If it's a break, use a screen splint, with screen and cord, but do not attempt to straighten the limb if it is in a bent position.

If the injury is incapacitating and persists in hurting, you have a problem but, if you have proceeded correctly up to this point, you may not have as much of a problem as you think. You should have a first aid handbook in your parka. Consult it.

Furthermore, back in the car, or wherever your tour started, you should have a toboggan, or at very least, a sled. A snow-

Extreme left: Lunch hike pack: traditional low profile Norwegian pack (left) with large outside pockets; taller American design center; small fanny pack for personal gear, front. Right: Day pack with large zippered map pocket in back.

mobile, of course, would be best, but even a kid's sled will do. Send someone for it. If it is a sled, tape or tie the injured person's skis to the runners, if need be, to keep the sled from sinking, and tow the person out.

If you should be caught with no sled, you can drag an injured skier out on a tarpaulin. But that won't be much fun.

You can buy a little "rescue sled kit" that fits in a backpack and converts a pair of skis into a rescue sled. This, of course, is an excellent solution, but is rather expensive when you consider the quite small chance of an injury this severe.

If you are not prepared at all, however, and somebody gets hurt, can't move out on his own, and has nothing warm to be rescued in, you can have a very serious problem. People who are injured sometimes go into shock and about the only thing you can do is keep them warm. To let them get cold is to risk their lives, literally, even though you have the means of getting them out.

We have gone quite far into the safety and rescue bit for a chapter on lunch hiking, but a day tour *can* mean being two or three hours deep in the woods. If you are the responsible leader, it will take a load off your mind to know you've made reasonably complete efforts to foresee the most frequent problems. If you meet one, you've got an answer.

A Lunch Hike Equipment List

On the other hand, you can't be prepared for *everything*. If someone is struck by lightning, you are not expected to be able to treat heavy burns, for instance.

Here's your equipment list:

map	pliers
flashlight	screwdriver
tarpaulin	small screws
wax kit	knife
first aid handbook	awl
moleskin, big bandaids	spare mittens

little bandaids
spare ski tip
spare pole basket
spare thong for replacing pole
   handle
plastic tape
roll of good cord
baling wire

spare socks
spare wool socks—toeless
candy bars or dextrose
aspirin
sun tan oil
spare sun glasses
screen

And, don't forget your toboggan, back at the starting point.

Using Autos on Day Tours

The automobile is usually what brings you out and what gets you back home from a day of touring.

There are some interesting ideas and some *caveats* in connection with cars.

You could do a "cross over" trip and have two groups, each leave a car at opposite ends of the trail. Exchange keys when you meet, and neither group will have to backtrack.

Today, you can rent a mobile camper, or perhaps you know someone who owns one. These are fantastic for group touring because they provide a place for warmth and food and sociability at the end of the day's tour.

However, your car can very easily be the vulnerable link in your tour plan if the car is not properly set up for winter. If you come back tired from a tour, and you are ten miles out on a country road and the car won't start, you have a big problem. You may have to ski out to civilization, assuming that it's not too far to reach.

You should, first of all, make sure your battery is charged up and will hold a charge. Your points and plugs should be checked frequently so the engine will catch quickly. Transistorized starting, which can be installed, will definitely help. Snow tires or studded tires are a must. Put a can of "dry gas" in the tank before you take off to get rid of any water in the gas. And make sure you have enough anti-freeze in the radiator.

If the weather is down toward zero, invest in a catalytic heater (runs on alcohol without a flame). When you return to the car, stick it under the hood near the battery, and cover the hood with a blanket. Wait half an hour before trying to start the car. Your car will start much more readily if the battery is warm. But as a further precaution, carry a can of "starting spray." If the car still won't start, take the filter off the carburetor and spray some directly into the carburetor as you try to start.

As winter operating equipment in the car, you should carry a set of clip-on chains for the drive wheels, a good shovel, and a bucket of sand or gravel for putting under a spinning wheel.

Make sure someone knows when you are supposed to be back, and where to come looking if you are not.

(If worse does come to worst, and no one shows up by nightfall, you are better off dragging the seats out of the car, digging snow caves in the snowbanks by the side of the road—if the banking is that high—or fashioning a snow-wall lean-to with a tarpaulin as roof. A metal car is about the coldest shelter you could have on a winter's night.)

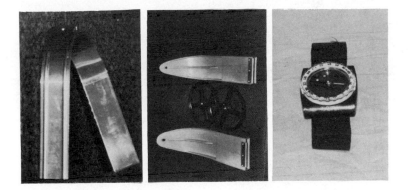

Left: Aluminum spare tip will scissor closed over broken tip and allow skier to continue. Center: Compact spare plastic tips and spare baskets are good emergency equipment for lunch hikes. Right: Silva waterproof wrist compass has orienteering card for alignment with map of a hike.

Capturing the Youth Vote

Day touring should mean fun and games.

Assuming you have children, and you want them to be part of your tour life, you have to include rewards other than those of physical exertion. (Kids get a lot of *that*.)

For three- to six-year-olds, plan a sort of graduated campaign to get them touring without making them feel it is a drag. Even in Norway, there are kids who resist all the cultural reinforcement (one out of three people skis), and simply refuse to learn. What at first is only an exercise of the individual's right to say no, may become a denial of a potentially rewarding part of one's adult recreational life.

First, plan trips that are short—half a mile at most—and predominantly downhill, and have a lunch waiting in a car at the end. No kid can resist the fun of gliding downhill; he'll even walk uphill to do it. (A prime mistake is to make a tour too long. Get them back while they're eager to continue.)

Play lots of games.

Follow The Leader is a great one, if you make sure the kids can rest if they get tired. Or cut up some black crepe paper and use it as markers for Fox and Hounds, dropping a mark every ten strides. (We are assuming that you are touring among other tracks—if not, the ski tracks themselves make fine markers.)

If you find a suitable hill, you can build a small bump and give candy mints as a reward for every spill-less jump made.

Pack your slope out by sidestepping and teach the kids snowplow turns (see Chapter Four). Give them parallel turns, if they start getting good.

One of the best ways to get kids hooked on touring is to shoot 8 mm. films and show them soon afterwards. Let *them* take a few pictures of you, too. Older kids respond better to adventure while younger kids respond well to the familiar with little variations.

For older kids, go find a new place. Show them how to get there with a map and perhaps make it a treasure hunt. (You can bury, ahead of time, things like a pocket knife or a compact). Once kids associate touring with pleasant times, the *inherent* rewards—going outdoors, reacting to the natural stimulants of exercise and cool crisp air and, for older kids, battling the challenges of steep hills, white snowstorms—will become self-reinforcing. You will soon have a family of tourers. (This doesn't necessarily mean that *everyone* has to tour every time anyone tours, however.)

Orienteering and Maps

For some groups, particularly large ones, the game of Orienteering, or going by compass over a pre-determined route against the clock, can be a lot of fun.

Orienteering is not only a game but a fine education in map reading and compass-following.

The best book on the subject, covering everything from map symbols to compass cross-bearings, is *Be Expert With Map and Compass,* by Bjorn Kjellstrom, which can be ordered from Silva Inc., La Porte, Indiana 46350.

A topographical map helps out in the game and adds immeasureable interest. Show it to everyone in the group; it makes people confident to know where they are. If you've never used a map like this before you will need experience in relating map contours to actual terrain. Topographical maps have contour rings, showing where each ten-foot rise above sea level is. The closer together the lines, the faster the hill rises or falls, however you travel it. Soon you will be able to look at a topographical map and pick out a reasonable way to go through country that you have not as yet skied.

Topographical maps can be purchased from a local book or outdoor store, or directly from the U.S. Geological Survey, 1200 South East Street, Arlington, Virginia 22202, in the United States; or from the Survey and Mapping Branch of the Department of Mines and Technical Surveys in Canada.

CHAPTER 8

Overnight on Tour Skis

Overnighting is essentially backpacking in winter. It is a reasonably esoteric experience: winter backpacking lags far behind summer backpacking as a popular sport. It is not as obviously attractive, or as easy. Nevertheless, anyone who has backpacked for a week in the summer can do the same in the winter, if he observes the differences carefully.

The biggest difference between winter and summer backpacking is the severity of the consequences. If you make mistakes in winter, you end up with a serious exposure problem.

The overnight ski tour needs, first of all, an experienced tour leader. He must be able to find his way in a storm, bivouac the group in the snow if necessary, and make sure he has the supplies and equipment to get in, stay in, and get out. In an extended tour in an unpopulated region—which is where the tour optimally goes—the leader must have a keen awareness of weather. Failure is not just a matter of broken bones, and a long trip out. It may mean no trip out.

A few winters ago, five Santa Monica tourers set off on a tour of the San Bernadino Mountains and hit a blizzard. They were not prepared either for accurate compass work or for an overnight in bad conditions. They lost their way and blundered into an impassable ravine. Their bodies were not found until spring. There were a number of ways in which they could have survived, but their leader had thought of none of them.

On the other hand, several hundred thousand skiers tour forty and fifty miles into the Norwegian mountains every winter. It is a special kind of touring, going from mountain inn to mountain inn, but everybody is practiced in doing it, and knows the limits and possibilities. The accidents are few and mild.

The key is experience.

This chapter could be expanded into a book very handily, and, in fact, there *are* books on winter outdoor camping listed in the appendix. The aim here is to point out in general what's needed for the experience and to go into some detail on equipment, which is the fastest changing aspect of winter camping today.

The return on your investment of time and care in overnight ski touring is beyond that of any other. The experience of being out on your own, super self-sufficient, going through some of the most silent and awesome surroundings that the planet can offer—this is unmatched by any other kind of tour experience, winter or summer.

Safety on the Far Snow

Safety is the basic parameter of winter overnight touring. Beyond all else safety lies in the ability—that comes only from experience—to weigh the gravity of a particular situation and keep your options open as long as possible. Another way of putting it: don't panic.

Chuck Malloy, who runs a fine winter camping program in Vail, Colorado, defines panic as "loss of common sense." You don't have to be screaming or sweating to be in a panic. You can be in a "calm panic" and make completely wrong-headed decisions. To keep cool-headed, you have to be able to withstand pressures generated by unusual situations.

The first rule of safety therefore, is never get tired. You can't think well when you are tired. Malloy has said, "A good mountaineer never breathes hard even. He's just never physically exhausted. If you do get tired, so that you have trouble keeping going, then you should rest and, if possible, get back to civilization again. Once you get that tired, you never regain your proper strength again on a continuing tour. If you can't get out, at least rest for a day."

The question of judgment and experience aside, the way to tour in safety lies in preparatory study and "dry-land" work. A good course in first aid is probably the rock-bottom preparation.

A course in snow-craft provided by one of the Forest Service divisions or a good amount of touring with really experienced guides is the only way to begin to know answers. If you don't know a lot about avalanches *stay out* of avalanche hazard areas. Your nearest Forest Service office will clue you in to dangerous areas.

Larsen

A well-laden overnight tourer heads into mountain country.

Hints for the Inexperienced Leader

You can avoid many possibly nasty situations by scouting locations in the summer and choosing one that is easy to get out of quickly, one where you can quickly get in touch with help, if need be. If this is done, you can go in as an inexperienced leader with the risk cut down to minimal size.

The question of water is tricky. Assure yourself that you'll have plenty of water at the site. (Check this again in winter because even a live stream can freeze or disappear.) If you plan a short stay, you can carry your water in. But make sure that your canteen is under your parka so it won't freeze. You will have a tough time making dinner at night if you have to unfreeze your water first.

The next necessity is fire. Small, light camp stoves are available, such as the Gerry *Mini-Stove,* fuel by propane and weighing only a pound. But you may not want to go to that expense until you are a confirmed winter camper. It is possible to scout out places where there is plenty of dry brush and dry dead wood. Don't *ever* count on sufficient firewood in a winter camping situation.

We shall leave out the food question here. It is rightfully given its own chapter after this one.

Disposal factors tie in with your supply of wood and water: You don't want your degradable garbage and toilet waste near your water supply, and you don't want to have to cut through the "dump" to get to your wood supply. A well set-up camp takes thinking. And scouting a place in summer is a way to do it.

Be sure to leave only degradable garbage. You do not leave anything at a winter campsite which won't be absorbed into the ground in the spring. Burn garbage before burying it in snow, if humanly possible. And do not leave tin cans, beer tops, bottles, aluminum foil or any plastic containers. Take them back with you. The outdoors is a shared experience but people don't want to share the sight of things you left behind.

Sleeping Well on Snow

If you freeze *one* night, it is enough. You need the same protection for one night as ten. Don't be fooled by the fact that you only plan a short stay. This takes a tent and sleeping gear.

The idea of building shelter is romantic: a snow cave, a lean-to or a brush hut, perhaps an igloo, all are somewhat impractical. For one thing, there are often not enough building materials in high country and, further, your sense of ecology may well tell you that this is not the place to take down trees. Even if there are plenty of trees, brush or snow, the building process is quite time-consuming; unless you have had plenty of experience in judging time and materials, a good tent is the answer. Furthermore, a good tent today weighs less than three pounds per person. A good two-man tent is the beginning of an enjoyable trip.

The old idea was that a tent should be waterproof—the new idea is that the tent should "breathe" and allow inside condensation to evaporate. Human beings expire about two pints of water each per night, just sleeping. If the tent is waterproof, the interior gets very clammy. Modern tents use a waterproof "fly" rigged to allow a few inches of air space above the tent roof to keep out the wet but let the roof "breathe."

New tents are nylon. Two-man tents weigh less than five pounds, including poles and suspension gear (and cost from $100 to $200). The lightest fly is made of reinforced polyethylene, and weighs eight ounces, for a 9' x 9'. A sturdier 9' x 12' plastic-coated nylon fly weighs two pounds. One new tent design is the Beelay Corporation's *Merrimac* ($185), which weighs seven pounds with fly. One whole side rolls up for good weather, or extends out as a "porch roof." Alpine Designs' *Timberline* ($100), and Gerry's *Year Around* ($90) are both excellent two-man tents of classic design.

Sleeping Bags

Modern sleeping bags contain the same kind of insulation as the old ones: goose down. But the new bags are cunningly sewn to trap the down and hold it in place, so a couple of pounds of down will do for the whole bag, and the bag will roll up into a ball no bigger than your head. Alpine Designs' *Nordic Sleeper* ($100) is all-nylon (except for the down), good to $-10°$, has a snap-in liner for easy cleaning, and joins a mate to zip into a double bag. Alpine has other models which go to as much as $-40°$.

Newly-fledged backpackers may contemplate a mattress of pine boughs. A two-inch thick foam mattress is superior, both ecologically and practically: it insulates against night time ground chill, cushions you against ridges and pebbles; and can be carried easily on top of your pack. Air mattresses are not recommended because they nearly always leak, and because they conduct ground chill directly to your body every time you shift your weight around.

Underneath your foam rubber mattress, you should have a waterproof ground cloth or tarpaulin.

Finally, you should have a double waterproof "stuff sack" for your down sleeping bag. Stuff the bag into one stuff sack, then into the other to guarantee a dry sleeping bag. Carry your foam pad on top of the pack: it insulates the whole pack, even when it is damp itself.

Back Packs

For an overnight trip, a two-part backpack is by far the best. The first part consists of the light frame that holds the pack comfortably on your back and distributes the load over the hips and shoulders.

The newest pack frames are North Face's one-piece injection-molded plastic frame ($15) which is extra-light (20 oz.), and flexes with body movements; and Alpine Designs' adjustable aluminum tube frame which can be fitted like a shoe to any size backpacker—with its wide padded waistband and extra-large backscreen it distributes the pack weight so well that any load carried feels five pounds lighter.

The second part of your pack rig is the pack sack itself: Like tents, pack sacks should not be waterproof but partly porous to

Larsen

Back packing in spring allows hikers to wear light clothes underway.

"breathe" and keep the contents from getting clammy. A pack cover wards off rain. Nylon packsacks are the lightest, and cost $30 and up.

Other Gear

Light aluminum and plastic cooking and serving sets that "nest" within each other to save space have been classic equipment for years, but the new type of cookstove is a development of the last three years. It is best exemplified by the 7-ounce Gerry *Mini-Stove,* which carries two and a half hours of cooking fuel in an innovative 6½-ounce *Mini Fuel* container: it reseals itself when detached after cooking. Another good model is the Primus *Grasshopper* propane stove, $9.50 including an eight-hour fuel cylinder.

Skis, Boots, and Bindings

There is great controversy in the area of winter ski camping equipment. Some people prefer skis and boots that are very much like Alpine equipment. They are willing to take the weight on their feet needed to bring them along, and the slow speed they necessitate.

The *trend* will be toward lighter ski equipment. In Scandinavia skiers are now using light touring gear for week-long hikes. The most important innovation in the field at this time is the fiberglass or metal-edge touring ski. Fischer makes a $65 mountain touring ski of fiberglass that has full-length edges and a $35 touring ski made of an aluminum sandwich. Both are unbreakable for all practical purposes and not much heavier than the general touring ski. Such skis promise to give the winter tour camper a whole new mode of transport. He'll be able to move faster, further, and get to camp less tired.

Because of their past tour experience, most high country tour leaders still prefer soft "powder" models of current metal skis, which are nearly unbreakable. If you are out in the high mountains in winter and your ski breaks, you are in big trouble. Added considerations: If you're not a good downhill skier on tour skis,

Touring party starts uphill in Colorado.

but are good on Alpine skis, and your route includes a large percentage of "hairy" downhills, you might rather sacrifice climbing ease for downhill security. The choice between wood cross-country skis and downhill metal skis depends greatly on the terrain you'll be meeting. As Chuck Malloy points out, "If you're touring in an area where the hills roll gently, as in Sweden you can get up and down them pretty easily but, in the Rockies, you're talking about slopes that are often straight up and down. You take your skis off and climb. You have to sometimes."

It's the same story with boots. You may find that general tour boots do not offer enough support when you are carrying a thirty-five-pound pack. They can also be cold when you stay in a ski camp in high mountain country for five hours or so. A reasonable compromise might be old leather Alpine ski boots, stiff enough to offer some support, but flexible enough to bend for touring. There is no really good solution as yet, however. As ski camping in the winter becomes more popular, boot manufacturers may put their heads together and come up with some warmer, more supportive but still flexible mountain tour boots.

Bindings are critical. If you put a general tour binding on an Alpine ski, and use heavier boots, you may bend the binding right off the ski. About the best binding is the Silvretta, which lets your heel come up. They're fairly lightweight for an Alpine binding, operate like a good cross-country binding, and they can take punishment without breaking right off the ski.

Clothing for Ski Camping

When you're going to be staying outdoors in wintertime overnight, clothing becomes more important. You will wear basically the same things you wear to day-tour, but there are some additions to include.

You must take long underwear, and be sure to take along a pair of wind pants. Two turtlenecks are recommended. You can dry one out at night, while wearing the other as a pajama top. You'll want a wool shirt or wool sweater over that, then a down parka. A good parka comes down at least six inches below the waist and has a strong plastic zipper and a drawstring at the bottom. You can always shed these layers as you need to avoid becoming overheated, but for longer-term tours in high country in wintertime, you must have it all on hand if a blizzard comes.

Take along a down hood. Forty percent of your body heat goes out from your head and neck (where you have your jugular vein and carotid artery) and there's only a thin covering of muscle to insulate it. To conserve heat you'll optimally wear a turtleneck, and scarf plus a wool hat.

The best thing to have for your hands are big, bulky down mittens; they conserve much more heat than anything else. You'll also need a pair of down booties for wearing inside your sleeping bag at night. If your gloves get wet and cold, the booties can double as hand protectors while you dry out your gloves inside your parka.

Overnighting can be just a breeze if you do things right, and one of the great things about it is making firm friends. The thought is not so conscious, perhaps, but should anything happen, the person beside you is part of your rescue. At the very least, there is a strong sense of companionship—and of expedition—even if you're only one mile from the road.

CHAPTER 9

The Winter Outdoor Chef

Fresh air, a good long bout of exercise, and several hours of brisk weather produces real "touring appetites." You'll want to carry tour food that satisfies without stuffing. You need to revive the tourers' energies without feeding them meals that take a long time to digest: at lunch you will soon be moving along again; at dinner you often go right to sleep rather shortly. Undigested food makes for bad sleep.

Beyond having energy-rich, easily-digested food, remember that meals while ski touring must be eminently *portable, storeable* and *easily prepared*. Finally, they have to taste good too—but more of that later.

The Three Big Requirements

Portability: You'll have to carry everything you need on your back—food, utensils, probably water and perhaps the stove and fuel. A light stove-and-fuel saves lots of time if you are going into an area where firewood is not plentiful—and dry. You may not even *want* to cut firewood as a matter of ecology.

Every excess pound on your back at the start of the tour calls for more energy to carry it, and therefore causes you to consume more food. Heavy foodstuffs are self-defeating in a tour pack. Portability is a must. You want food that is *compact* for the energy it gives.

Storeability: You're going to be out in the wilds without any dependable refrigeration. There's snow to use as a coolant, but temperatures can rise fast enough to make snow useless. And snow wets your food containers. Tour food, therefore, should not require refrigeration and, further, it should stand being heated by the sun without spoiling.

Ease of preparation: You should keep preparation and cooking time to a minimum. The longer you spend cooking, the more fuel you use up. It's time-consuming to clean pots in the winter outdoors where hot water is a luxury. Keep the pots used to one or two if possible. The longer you cook and clean, the less time you have to relax. It's more fun to spend your time contemplating mountains, birds, animal tracks, evergreens, blue sky and evening stars than crouching at the campfire.

The Importance of Planning

Whether it's to be a lunch hike or a week's trek: plan ahead. And check, check, check! You'll be repaid a thousandfold. To avoid just one bagatelle like forgetting a corkscrew, is worth the pain of meticulous planning. A quickly-fed, well-fed crew of tourers is a happy, relaxed group: that's what you came for.

Begin before the tour by planning a menu for each meal, each day. Make a "buy list" from the total menu plan. Then check off each item as you pack it. There is no going back to the supermarket.

The menu plan is super-useful if the chef gets a bad cold and is not in shape to cook. Anyone can be substitute-cook and get it all together without completely destroying the overall plan if a menu is written down to follow.

Planning your menus beforehand means you will know what you're going to serve; you can't expect to be inventive after putting out a lot of energy touring.

Basic Nutrition

"Camping cookbooks" often neglect balanced nutrition on the theory you're not going to be out there long enough to ruin your health. True, you're not going to get scurvy, but lack of the proper amounts of the proper nutrients *can* cause problems even on a short term basis.

Vitamins: People under stress may require several times the normal daily requirement of a particular vitamin. Lack of sufficient vitamins fouls up your physical motor and can make you irritable and draggy: you won't tour as easily. Processed and ready-prepared foods *are* storeable and portable but are often low in vitamins. (It's hard to retain them through a number of processing steps.)

Take a bottle of high-potency, multi-vitamin mineral-supplement tablets with you. Make everyone take some. They offer great insurance in a small space when it comes to maintaining health and vigor.

Roughage: Your intestinal system needs some indigestible fibers to work and function correctly. Take along dried fruit and whole fresh vegetables: celery, carrots, beets, and coarse whole-grain bread or bran cereal.

Water and salt: Touring causes you to perspire up to two pints of water a day, and "body salt" goes out with perspiration in the natural cooling process.

You must replace this water and salt or you will become dehydrated, a very uncomfortable state. Serve some salted food every day. Take in plenty of liquid in small doses throughout the day (don't fill up your stomach with liquid all at once, then let it stay dry for three hours). For lack of canteen water, you can try the "old guide method" of eating handfuls of snow as

Heavy exercise breeds hearty appetites on a tour.

you go along. But be very sure you allow the snow to melt and warm in your mouth before swallowing. A sudden jolt of ice water in your insides can give you cramps.

Sugar: To save bulk keep sugar to a minimum. The average person touring should not need endless doses of pure sugar or candy bars to get needed energy. Dextrose tablets for a pick-up are fine if someone is suffering a real lag in spirits, but most of us get enough energy (carbohydrate) from our regular diet if it includes bread, vegetables, fruits, potatoes, jam.

Protein: You can't go wrong eating protein on a tour: eggs, cheese, lean meat, etc. It's the one nutrient your body must have every day to replace worn out cells. If you really have an energy-food shortage, your body can convert protein to energy forms.

Taste: All non-perishable foods *can* taste great. Almost everything that comes freeze-dried, dehydrated or keeps naturally can be made palatable by adding a little spice here and there.

The Freeze Dry Revolution

In the past five years there has been a revolution in freeze-dried and dehydrated foods. Companies such as Rich-Moor, Mountain House and Dri-Lite offer complete lines from shrimp cocktail to Beef Stroganoff, from cherry pie to chocolate pudding. Freeze-dried foods are the lightest and most compact of all foods: a half pound of meat, after freeze-drying, weighs only two ounces.

Freeze-dried foods *are* expensive: chicken stew for four persons is $2.95. You do buy a pretty tasty complete meal. The new freeze-dried foods are *not at all* like those powdered eggs they had years ago. You just add boiling water and let the freeze-dried meal sit for a few minutes. It's ready. And these meals *are* compact: chicken stew weighs nine ounces. Freeze-dried foods last indefinitely when kept dry. You're only out touring for a relatively short period of time: the convenience probably overrides the cost factor.

There are ways of combatting cost, too. Many standard supermarket items make excellent tour food: dehydrated soups, macaroni-and-cheese dinners, concentrated breakfast cereals (such as Grape-Nuts or Kellogg's Concentrate), dried fruits, noodles with dry sauce ingredients included, flavored rice mixes, even dehydrated omelettes with diced ham, chives, onion or bacon bits.

Remove the bulky, non-protective packages and re-wrap these foods in plastic bags or aluminum foil pouches. Be sure to save the directions where necessary and identify the packages with waterproof labels and marker pen.

Supermarket items to look for:

- instant or freeze-dried *coffee*
- *tea* bags, or instant tea with lemon and sweetener already added
- *bouillon,* cubes or powders
- instant "cup-a-*soup*"
- concentrated *drink mixes* (lemonade, Kool-Aid, etc.: add powdered saccharin to unsweetened drinks instead of sugar to save bulk)
- dehydrated *vegetable flakes:* mixed and in single varieties, including parsley, onion, celery, green pepper
- instant *cocoa* with milk and sugar in it
- instant *potatoes:* mashed or in "bud" form, and in mixes, scalloped, hashed brown, creamed, shoestring
- dry-roasted *nuts* (won't spoil)
- *wheat germ* (an excellent source of protein, vitamins, and iron): add to hamburgers, meat loaf, scrambled eggs, one-pot meals, fruits; eat as a cereal
- instant *milk,* powdered non-dairy *creamer*
- *spices and seasonings:* powdered mustard, horseradish, chili powder, dried mint leaves (add to tea for a refreshing drink), salt, pepper, garlic powder, dried mushrooms, cinnamon, a whole nutmeg, a couple of vanilla beans
- dry *gravy mixes* and *sauce mixes*
- instant *pudding* (the "shaker" type)
- *gelatin desserts:* good hot as a beverage as well as cold if you have the time
- instant *breakfast drinks* like Tang (in two flavors)
- instant *rice* and seasoned rice mixes

- the new "complete" *pancake mixes* (all you add is water)
- *biscuit and muffin mixes* (the add water-only kind)
- canned *bacon:* tastes so good it's worth the weight; also dry "Baco Bits"
- dried *fruits:* prunes, raisins, apricots, peaches, pears, dates, mincemeat (a good raw concentrated food)
- *candy:* hard fruit drops, "M 'n M's", etc.
- *cheeses:* natural ones (cheddar, Swiss, provolone, Monterey Jack, gouda, grated parmesan and romano, edam, caciocavallo, gjetöst, etc.) The best ones are "hard," or with a "skin"
- *crackers, toast:* melba type, unleavened breads
- *instant hot cereals:* many come with fruit or sugar and cinnamon added, plus good old Cream of Wheat, etc.
- *sandwich spreads:* "deli spreads" need no refrigeration

Best Cooking Methods

It *is* possible to bake, poach, stew and deep-fry outdoors, but it's best to stick with simple boiling, broiling and pan-frying to save time and energy.

Broiling is the easiest way of all: put small pieces of food on green sticks or metal brochettes over an open fire.

Boiling (and simmering): a deep skillet is the best single all-around utensil. You can do one-dish meals in a large deep skillet; it can also be used for breakfasts of bacon and flapjacks.

Pan sautéing: use a hydrogenated vegetable fat or regular margarine. Both heat to higher temperatures than butter without smoking, and both can be kept without refrigeration.

Meat can be pan-fried *without* fat, even without a teflon pan. "Salt fry" it. Put some salt in your pan and heat. When the salt starts to turn brown, drop in the meat. The salt will help sear it and seal in the juices.

By all means, make your meals one-pot meals which prepare quickly and use less fuel; there's something soul-satisfying about a big pot full of warm, fragrant, filling food. Small-cut vegetables, stewed fruits, freeze-dried food, omelettes and hot cereals all cook easily in a deep skillet.

A super trick: fix several vegetables in the same pot without mixing them. Cut the vegetables into small pieces (matchsticks, cubes, slivers, chunks, diagonal slices, etc.) and place inside aluminum foil packets with a dab of butter, some salt and pepper. Wrap tightly and drop the packets into the pot of boiling water. If you vary the size of the pieces you cut according to the length of time the vegetable ordinarily takes to cook (long cookers get smaller pieces, short ones larger), you'll get them all done at the same time in the same skillet or pot. (It won't even need cleaning when you're through.)

Pre-mix and pre-package most of the meals. Mix dehydrated vegetable-beef soup, some dehydrated vegetable flakes (onions, carrots, celery), a package of freeze-dried meatballs, and instant potato flakes (for thickening) in the proper quantities at home; package it carefully in tightly wrapped foil and it's ready to be popped into a pot of boiling water, and simmered for a few minutes into a delicious stew. No fumbling around measuring and mixing on the trail.

This technique applies to breakfast just as handily: mix proper quantities of cold cereal, raisins, powdered milk, sugar. Add hot water to serve. You might package your mix in individual plastic bags, each one holding one portion.

The Lunch Hike

For a lunch hike, make sure you've included *enough* food. You probably have people who came along primarily because they envisioned a picnic under the blue sky and warm sun and have been thinking of food ever since they strapped on their skis. You'll meet all expectations with an assortment of cold cuts, cheeses, fruit, dark bread and some wine, chocolate bars and cookies.

Take a lot of non-alcoholic beverages along also. You are better off slaking everyone's thirst with non-alcohols at mid-morning break and saving the wine for a taste treat at lunch. Remember, too much wine will throw everyone's coordination off, turning the trip into a tiresome trek afterwards.

Cheese fondue is another good lunch hike menu. A fondue is excellent outdoors, no matter how primitive the preparation.

Melt good gruyere cheese and stir in wine over a very moderate fire. (Keep the pot off the flames; take it away entirely if the fondue starts to burn.) Let each person find his own twig, tear up the bread into chunks (if you do it beforehand it gets stale) and dip the bread. Using sticks, there's a good chance that someone will lose his bread in the pot, and the old Swiss fondue custom (the boy who loses his bread has to kiss the girl at his right, or vice versa) can be well-observed.

Oranges are one of the best all-around trail snacks possible: they quench the thirst, have high energy content and are always fresh.

Menus for Overnight Tours

On tours of more than a day, plan simple trail lunches rather than the elaborate one above. A cup of hot bouillon makes a welcome starter for any lunch. The water and salt in bouillon, plus the warmth, acts as an excellent pick-me-up.

Follow with "gorp," ready-to-eat high-energy foods, made by mixing any or all of the following: raisins, dates, figs, or other dried fruit; cubes of hard cheese; bacon bars, compressed meat bars, or beef jerky; chocolate candies, preferably the no-melt-in-your-hand-variety; hard candies; small cocktail-type crackers. Gorp has several advantages: you eat a small volume so you don't fill your stomach up with a large, slowly digested meal (digestion takes a lot of blood away from your extremities and brings it to your stomach), and you don't take lots of time out for the noontime meal.

One of the most rewarding things to carry on the trail is a thermos of hot cocoa, tea or bouillon. It makes a great midmorning and mid-afternoon snack, along with oranges and gorp. Another good idea is to give everyone some instant fruit-flavored drink powder and a paper cup for mixing "instant sherbet" from the snow when the group takes a break.

One-Pot Trail Dinner

Here's a typical dinner to cook in one pot, one that will come out tasting great: bouillon appetizers with Triscuits, pork chops with apple slices, carrots, flavored rice, coffee, chocolate candy.

How is it done? With freeze-dried foods and foil and three bowls. Heat a large kettle of boiling water. Place the freeze-dried pork chops in one bowl (previously lined with aluminum foil) and put dehydrated apple slices on top. Place seasoned instant rice mix in the second bowl (adding extra dehydrated celery and onion, salt and pepper to taste); put freeze-dried carrots in the third. Add the proper amount of boiling water to each dish, cover, and let steep for the required number of minutes. Take the whole bowlful of pork chops and apple slices and wrap tightly into a package (with several layers of foil if necessary). Place the package over the heat source to brown a bit. Add a spoon of sugar to the carrots to make them taste fresher and more tender. Meanwhile, leave enough water in the pot to make cups of bouillon (put powdered or cube bouillon in each cup), and after-dinner coffee (with the addition of the proper amount of freeze-dried coffee).

Menu Plan

Here's a typical menu plan for four people on a weekend ski tour (two days):

Saturday Breakfast

Grape-Nuts with raisins, sugar, powdered milk

Instant orange breakfast drink (Tang)

Bacon bars (dried, compressed)

Coffee (freeze-dried) with sugar and non-dairy creamer

Sunday Breakfast

Reconstituted dried apricots

Freeze-dried omelette with bacon bits

Ry-Krisp with canned butter & jam

Instant breakfast drink

Coffee with sugar and non-dairy creamer

Saturday Lunch

(Trail Lunch)
Hot bouillon from thermos
  (make in morning)
Gorp

Sunday Lunch

Freeze-dried beef stew
Instant cocoa
Instant potatoes with grated
  cheese topping
Fresh oranges/candy

Saturday Dinner

Freeze-dried Beef Stroganoff
Noodles with canned butter
Puff-dried carrot slices with salt
  & lemon crystals
Fresh celery sticks

Reconstituted pears (dried) with
  cinnamon
Cheddar cheese/dry roasted nuts
Coffee with sugar and non-dairy
  creamer

More tasty and satisfying one-pot meals:

Skillet Paella

Saffron-flavor rice mix
Freeze-dried peas
Dehydrated onion, celery, and
  tomato flakes
Freeze-dried chunk chicken
Freeze-dried tuna fish
  (or canned if you can afford
  the extra weight)
Can of cooked small shrimp

Add proper amount of boiling
water to rice mix, allow to steep
a few minutes, then add freeze-
dried food and proper amounts
of boiling water, steep another
few minutes, add shrimp. Serve.

One-Pot Ham Casserole

Dehydrated instant sweet pota-
  toes
Dehydrated diced ham
Freeze-dried chunky pineapple
Brown sugar
Cinnamon

Add proper amount of boiling
water to reconstitute the ham,
sweet potatoes and pineapple.
Layer into pot: 1) sweet potatoes, 2) ham, 3) pineapple.
Sprinkle each layer with brown
sugar and cinnamon. Heat gently
a minute and serve.

Special Chicken Pot

Dehydrated chicken chunks
Freeze-dried peas
Slivered dry-roasted almonds
Dried mushrooms, dry cream
  sauce mix
Instant "chicken flavor" rice mix
  (or instant rice plus chicken
  bouillon cube, dehydrated onions, poultry seasoning, salt,
pepper)

Add proper amounts of boiling
water to reconstitute the chicken,
peas, and mushrooms. Prepare
sauce, rice mix. Layer in a pot:
1) rice, 2) chicken and vegetables, 3) sauce, and 4) almonds.
Serve.

CHAPTER 10

Racing
Cross-Country

Fritjof Nansen, the Norwegian polar explorer, once skied 240 miles over rough, unexplored terrain in nineteen days and eventually made it across Greenland from coast to coast. He spoke of cross-country in glowing terms: "I know of no form of sport which renders the body so strong and elastic, which teaches so well the qualities of dexterity and resourcefulness, which in equal degree calls for decision and resolution, and which gives the same vigor and exhilaration to mind and body alike. . . ."

The rationale for racing has never been better stated. It is far the best way for an experienced tourer to improve technique. Advances in technique made in racing are often passed down in the form of better ways to tour.

But there is a danger in dwelling too much on racing. The *teaching* of touring requires a frame of reference wholly different from cross-country racing. To introduce racing exercises and difficult terrain at the beginner level may discourage people of good will and sufficient leisure from continuing to tour. The first day frightens them. It is exactly this confusion of touring and racing that has held back touring in this country.

Alpine skiing has had the same problems. But, the advent of short skis in Alpine ski teaching (the Graduated Length Method—GLM—which *Ski Magazine* has promoted with great success) has led to a whole new approach; GLM is being applied at well over 100 ski resorts in this country. The ethic of Alpine *racing* which interfered with the proper teaching of Alpine skiing for decades is slowly giving way to a more intelligent teaching ethic.

An analogous revolution is starting to take hold in tour skiing. The racing ethic is being divorced from teaching touring to beginners. No longer are first day pupils urged to spring around the track in imitation of the Nordic racer. They are counseled to take their time, enjoy the view, and make their tour more of a hike than a race. They are being motivated to continue in the sport by being allowed to enjoy the first day.

A couple of 60-year olds get ready to run in Sweden's Vasaloppet race.

The Advantages of Racing

Cross-country ski racing is lots of fun, however. You don't necessarily have to be very good or very experienced to enjoy racing. This may seem to contradict the foregoing, but, if the skier is strong, young and/or already an experienced athlete with plenty of endurance racing will help him enjoy touring.

Today there exist a number of very easy-going races around the country. The "mass race" or "citizens' race," for example, resembles a hare-and-hounds game at a picnic. Twenty to two hundred people leave the starting line together on a wide race track, the so-called "geschmozzle start," and first man home is the winner.

The classic cross-country race, on the other hand, has a staggered start with skiers going off at intervals, and racing against the clock. A good racer will pass the men ahead and the men overtaken have to step aside in the track and let the fast racer go by. The most organized of the classic races for the ordinary skier are NASTAR or National Standard Races, which are held under the auspices of the NASTAR organization, originated by *Ski Magazine* for Alpine and Nordic racing.

The goal of NASTAR is the establishment of a nationally valid handicap for each racer. The resorts participating every winter in NASTAR each send their own "pace-setter" to the national pace-setting trials early in the season. Each resort's pace-setter then receives a handicap in relation to the "scratch time," that of the best pace-setter of them all. The day of a NASTAR event, the pace-setter's time for the course is compared to your time across the same course and, by some elementary figuring, your own national handicap can be computed. In effect, everybody knows how his result rates against what the best racer in the country would have done over this particular course. This precisely is the way a golf handicap tells the individual golfer how he rates against a "par," the scratch performance for that particular course.

There are a number of other racing organizations in addition to NASTAR; American colleges have an intercollegiate racing circuit; there is a United States Ski Association Nordic Team,

whose members are the best cross-country racers and ski jumpers in the nation. Compared to Europe, our Nordic competitors
are a second-level team but we keep trying. Occasionally, we
put a man in fourth or fifth at the big European meets. That's
nothing to be ashamed of, because we are just beginning to get
interested. Someday we may race cross-country as well as the
Europeans. There's hope that as the popularity of touring and
cross-country racing increases, the base from which to pick
racers will grow.

Racing Technique

The difference between the touring skier and the cross-country
racer is 1) the lightness of his equipment and 2) the speed
with which he executes his stride motions.

Current cross-country racing skis weigh about half as much
as pre-1950 racing skis. Modern racing and light touring skis
are beautifully crafted, expensive, and breakable on rough terrain. Light weight is extremely important to good results. The
racer must treat his skis tenderly even during the race.

Modern racing technique stresses a flowing movement. The
arm and leg extend farther forward and farther back than in
regular touring. The stride is kicked off explosively and yet the
skier has to move smoothly from kick to kick; the best skier is
the man who best combines smoothness, power, and quick, sure
movements. It's not simply brute power that wins.

The movement in cross-country is a willful, driving tempo with
the body muscles alternately driving and relaxing like a good
long distance runner's legs. The cross-country racer pays close
attention to the efficiency of all body movements: nothing is
superfluous.

The arms move in a pendulum nearly straight back and forth
in line with the direction of the skier's travel. The hand passes
close to the hip as it drives the pole backward and comes close
again as, relaxed, it swings forward to plant the pole.

Arms that swing close to the body are much more efficient
in utilizing the drive from the pole than an arm held out to
the side a bit. The straighter back the push, the more directly
the impelling force of the pole shoves the skier forward.

Uphill striding in race conditions: the key to uphill is keeping the smooth flowing motions of the diagonal form without undue up and down motions, and compensating for a much shorter glide. On steep terrain, of course, there will be no glide at all.

To avoid superfluous movement, the racing skier watches that his upper body stays between the skis, and does not bob heavily from ski to ski in an exaggerated weight shift. This idea has only belatedly been recognized in the United States. One of the disadvantages racers in this country have had is that they had all been (some still are) taught to shift weight completely *over* one ski and then completely over the other ski: as one ski went forward, the head and shoulders followed that ski. The exaggerated side-to-side movement that results is far less efficient than a more limited movement of the body *in between* the skis.

Another common mistake is to allow the head to bob up and down when the skier tries for speed; this means he is using strength to raise and lower the body, a movement that does not contribute to forward speed. The experienced cross-country racer (and the experienced fast tourer, too) will have smooth knee-bending coordination to keep his head moving at almost the same level above the snow during the alternation of one ski and the next.

Solvang

Two skiers using an uphill racing stride during a tour. Even though there is very little glide going uphill, the "diagonal" form persists, with the hand on one side and knee on the other going forward together.

Brady

A study of up-grade technique: Galina Koulacova of the U.S.S.R. is the 1972 Olympic triple gold medalist at Sapporo. Note the relaxed near hand bringing the pole forward.

The racer and fast tour skier will concentrate their strength on driving the knee forward to its limit. It's wrong to slack the drive of the knee as the forward-moving knee passes the other knee moving back. The racer's ability to drive the knee forward a greater distance than the untrained tour skier can is one of the distinct traits that racing develops.

Breathing, which may seem a natural enough movement, has also to be changed from normal intake to a much more studied intake-exhale bringing fresh oxygen supplies to the blood as quickly as possible.

Poling Technique in Racing

The cross-country racer gets a good deal more propulsion out of his arms than the ordinary tour skier. The racer, for one thing, has painstakingly built his arms up with month-long routines of various strength exercises. While most untrained skiers' legs are naturally quite strong, (it is pretty hard to walk without continually exercising them), the average non-racer's arms are relatively puny. Nothing similar to walking is demanded of his arms day after day.

The modern cross-country racer uses his arm strength to put his pole in with a slightly bent arm (more power than if fully extended in front); he then gives one great sustained shove downward and back—all the way back—to extract the last shred of forward speed out of the arm movement.

A racer will double-pole when the conditions are right or when he feels he needs a change of rhythm to rest the muscles. Going over the crest of a hill onto the down slope, for instance, the racer normally starts to double pole and keeps doing it as long as he feels he doesn't have more speed than he can handle down the hill. When he comes to a downhill turn, he'll skate around it, trying to thrust with his leg at each skating step to keep his speed up.

When he's reached what he considers a suitable top speed for the hill in question, the racer will go into a "tuck," putting his forearms down on his knees and ducking his head to reduce wind resistance on the way down.

The most dramatic difference between the tour skier and the cross-country racer, however, is in uphill technique.

The tour skier is usually content if his skis hang in there and don't slip back. He doesn't hurry up a hill. The racer *runs* uphill, shortening and speeding up his stride, going up on his toes at the end of the stride, thrusting deliberately *down* into the snow as well as forward on the kick motion, to nail the ski to the slope. The racer's uphill technique is a sort of inspired *jogging* movement. It takes strength and will. You must admire a man who has gone thirty miles and three hours and yet blithely runs up a hill in perfect form *in spite of fatigue;* only intensive training can produce this kind of performance.

Cross-Country Events

The classic cross-country distances are the men's 5 kilometer, 15 kilometer, 30 kilometer and the 50 kilometer; women run the 5 kilometer and the 10 kilometer. One United States mile is about 1.6 kilometers, so the men's races are roughly 3 miles, 10 miles, 20 miles, and 30 miles. A top racer can average 10 miles an hour over 20 miles: this is approximately the speed of an Olympic winner, give or take a number of tenths due to the conditions.

The physical condition of top cross-country racers is phenomenal. A team of doctors who once measured the energy output required in various sporting events determined that the most demanding of the commonly practiced sports in the world is cross-country racing.

Scandinavians have greater reverence than Americans for endurance races. For instance, they never allow their ten-year-olds to race more than 2 kilometers, about 3.2 miles, and then only after having carefully trained them at shorter distances to condition their entire systems to appreciate the distance. It probably wouldn't do the average ten-year-old much harm to run until he dropped of exhaustion. Ten-year-olds are notoriously resilient.

Brady

Teyck Weed, U.S.A., in the 1970 World Championships in Tatry, Czecho-
slovakia, going all-out on the flat.

Above: Start of the women's relay race at Holmenkollen, Norway in the 1971 Holmenkollen competition.

Below: Paul Tydum of Norway on his way to a gold medal in the 1972 Olympic 50 kilometer race at Sapporo, Japan.

But it would be against the Scandinavian *idea*: distance racing is a distinct privilege that the skier is granted only after proving his desire and willingness to train. The long distance ski runner is the Scandinavian equivalent of our pro football hero.

Training Methods

The serious racer trains year round.

First of four highly developed phases is "interval training" in which the racer runs or skis distances considerably shorter than his final race but at great speed. This builds up his "anaerobic capacity," or tolerance for oxygen debt. A ski racer needs a strong kick up the hill; he catches up on his breathing on the downhill or at the finish after the line is crossed. A very technical interval training schedule alternates intense activity intervals of five minutes, which can be repeated two to ten times, with shorter activity intervals of a minute or less, which are repeated with intervening rest periods as much as sixty times.

"Tempo training" is a second phase. The racer runs a tenth or a fifth of his normal racing distance at high speed to learn to build tolerance to the waste products produced by bodily exertion.

In "distance training," on the other hand, the racer over-runs his distance by as much as half, to build up aerobic capacity.

Finally, in "strength-building training," the racer strengthens the muscles most called-upon in cross-country events by means of selected exercises, such as weight lifting.

The four phases of training should be varied in frequency according to the time of year. The racer builds to a peak for the races at the end of the winter season when the world, national and regional championships are up.

Training for serious cross-country racing is a matter of proven meticulous programming. No one unwilling to submit to this discipline, and furthermore, to *enjoy* it on the whole, should think he's ready for national cross-country racing.

The "civilian" racer need not be quite so serious. The main thing is that he also enjoy it. It will help him better his general technique because better technique pays off visibly in racing. And he will be inspired to make some effort at training between races so he can assure himself that a race is not merely a winding-down-to-exhaustion kind of thing but, rather, a thoroughly tough but rewarding high-capacity activity. The tourer will thus become a stronger, better skier through cross-country racing.

The racing diagonal stride. This is much the same as the touring diagonal stride but the arms push harder, emphasize a close-to-the-body swing, and the stride is longer and faster, with the leg straightening out more decisively after the kick. The weight goes fully on the "driving knee" (third picture) as it moves forward into the glide. The skier does not, however, shift his weight *over* the gliding ski. He bounds toward it and rebounds onto the other ski, staying between the skis.

The racing skating turn. Note how, in contrast to the more leisurely touring skating turn, the racer kicks himself quickly from the ski in the track to the ski going in the new direction (third picture). His kicking leg is almost straight as he shifts weight quickly to the ski going in the new direction.

The racing uphill stride. The skier has *some* glide to the ski, unlike the tour skier, who is largely satisfied just to stride uphill. The racing skier pushes *down* as well as forward as he kicks, to help keep the ski from backsliding. His head is low and forward, always ahead of the driving knee, so that the maximum thrust is always on this forward ski. He may lift the back ski slightly in moving it forward to help the uphill jogging movement.

APPENDIX

Ski Touring and Cross-Country Racing Organizations

Ski Touring Council, Inc.
342 Madison Avenue, Room 727
New York, New York 10017

National Director
United States Nordic Program
United States Ski Association (USSA)
1726 Champa Street, Suite 300
Denver, Colorado 80202

Director of Recreation and Membership
Ski Touring Program
United States Ski Association
(address same as above)

Director of Ski Touring
Far West Ski Association, (USSA)
812 Howard Street
San Francisco, California 94103

Central Division
Ski Touring Council, Inc.
4437 First Avenue South
Minneapolis, Minnesota 55409

Rocky Mountain Division
Ski Touring Council, Inc.
Mount Werner Training Center
Steamboat Springs, Colorado 80477

NASTAR (National Standard Races)
World Wide Ski Corporation
240 Madison Avenue
New York, New York 10016

or

World Wide Ski Corporation
2305 Canyon Boulevard
Boulder, Colorado 80302

Where to Write For Ski Touring Information and Lessons

For information on where to tour, trails, guided tours, races, maps, lessons write to the following:

Ski Touring Council, Inc., 342 Madison Avenue, Room 727, New York, New York 10017.

The Ski Touring Council has information on trails throughout the United States and Canada. Write and ask for their guide which is available for $1.00 and their schedule of current activities for $1.50.

California:	*Yosemite Mountaineering,* Yosemite Park & Curry Co., Yosemite National Park, Calif. 95389
Colorado:	Steve Rieschl, *Vail Ski Touring School,* Vail, Colo. Rod Hanson, *Nordic Ski Tours,* P.O. Box 608, Carbondale, Colo. 81623 *Lars Larsen,* P.O. Box 88, Aspen, Colo. 81611 *Ashcroft Ski Tours Unlimited,* Ashcroft Ober Aspen, Box 1572, Aspen, Colo. 81611
Idaho:	*Sun Valley Nordic Ski School,* Sun Valley, Idaho 83353
Michigan:	*Skicrosse Touring Club,* 135 Albertson St., Rochester, Mich. 48063
Minnesota:	*North Star Ski Touring Club,* 4231 Oakdale Ave. S., Minneapolis, Minn. 55416
New Hampshire:	*Akworth Cross-Country Inn,* Akworth, N. H. 03601 *Dartmouth Outing Club,* Hanover, N. H. 93755
New York:	*Williams Lake Resort Area,* Rosendale, N. Y. 12472 *Lake Placid Touring Program,* Lake Placid Chamber of Commerce, Lake Placid, N. Y. 12946
Pennsylvania:	*Kinzua Country,* Kinzua Dam Vacation Bureau, 305 Market St., Warren, Pa. 16365 Forest Supervisor, *Allegheny National Forest,* U. S. Forest Service, Post Office Building, Warren, Pa. 16365
Vermont:	*Putney Ski Club,* Putney, Vt. 05346 *Trapp Family Lodge,* Stowe, Vt. 05832 *Burke Mountain Recreational Area,* East Burke, Vt. 05832 *Sugarbush Inn,* Warren, Vt. 05674 *Stratton Mountain,* Stratton, Vt. 05155 *Woodstock Inn,* Woodstock, Vt.

The author (above) and Paul Ryan (facing page), making *Ski Touring Is For People* for Garcia Ski Corp., a 12½ minute color film with live on-camera sound.

Canada:

Ski Touring Division, *Canadian Amateur Ski Association*, P.O. Box 2566, Station D, Ottawa, Ontario

Hans Gmoser, *Canadian Mountain Holidays,* 132 Banff Ave., P.O. Box 583, Banff, Alberta
Canadian Mountain Holidays offers exciting ski touring and extended glacier ski tours at Rogers Pass in Glacier National Park and on Mt. Assiniboine, as well as in the Cariboo Mountains.

Where to Tour

EAST
Connecticut:
Mt. Riga plateau, Salisbury
People's State Forest, Barkhamsted
Tunxis State Forest and Granville State Forest, Hartlands
White's Woods, Litchfield

Massachusetts:
Hoosac range circuit, North Adams
Petersburg Pass, Berlin Mountains, Berlin
Pittsfield State Forest, Pittsfield
Taconic Range
Williams College, Williamstown

Maine:
Acadia National Park, Mt. Desert Island
Freyburg (racing trail)
Squaw Mountain, Greenville

Maryland:
Savage River State Forest

New Hampshire:
Bear Mountain State Park, Allenstown
Crawford Notch area
Dartmouth area, Hanover
Franconia-Mittersill area
Greeley Pond Trail
Gulf of Slides Trail, White Mountain National Forest
Jackson area
Jaffrey
Mittersill ski area
Pinkham Notch, Mt. Washington, Gorham
Waterville Valley, Waterville

New Jersey:
Great Gorge, McAfee
High Point State Park
Stokes State Forest

New York:
Adirondack Mountains—sites include Old Forge, Black Bear Mountain, Lake Placid region, Mt. Vanhoevenberg area, Long Lake, Lake Colden, Avalanche Lake, Duck Hole, the Preston Ponds, Mt. Marcy, Keene Valley area, Whiteface, Arietta region (Trout Lake)
Allegheny State Park
The Ausable Lakes
Bavarian Haus Berg, Pauling
Bear Mountain, Palisades Interstate Park
Belleayre, Highmount

Big Bear, Vega
Big Tupper, Tupper Lake
Bonticou Winter Park, New Paltz
Capital District—various sites in Albany-Troy-Schenectady area
Catskills—includes Slide Mountain, Lake Minnewaska, Lake Mohonk, Mt. Tremper, Partridge Run Game Area, Rosendale
Charleston State Park, Amsterdam
Crown Point—Miller Mountain, Knob Pond, Overshot Pond
Genesee Valley
Gore Mountain, North Creek
Greek Peak, Cortland
Hammondville
Harriman Interstate Park
Harvey Mountain, North River
Holiday Mountain, Monticello
Holiday Valley, Ellicottville
Hunter Mountain, Hunter
John Boyd Thatcher State Park
Juniper Hills, Harrisville
Lake George area
Lake Placid area
Lake Sebago
Paleface, Wilmington
Palisades Interstate Park
Peek 'n Peak, Clymer
Pound Ridge Reservation, Cross River
Rensselaerville—Cheese Hill Reforestation area
Rockland Lake
St. Lawrence University Snow Bowl, Canton
Schroon Lake
Slide Mountain
Snow Ridge, Turin
Speculator
Taconic region—Cherry Plains game-management area
Wallkill Park

Wells region
West Mountain, Glens Falls

Pennsylvania:
Camelback, Tannersville
Delaware Water Gap, Kittatinny Mountains
Devil's Hole, Mt. Pocono region
Elk Mountain, Uniondale
Hamburg area
Hickory State Park, Whitehaven
Pocono Mountains
Tafton

Vermont:
Ames Hill to South Pond
Marlboro—Brattleboro area
Burrington Hill, Whitingham
Dunville Hollow and Burgess Road Trail, Bennington
Burke Mountain, East Burke
Long Trail, Big Branch, Danby
Glen Ellen, Waitsfield
Jay Peak, North Troy
Long Trail—Manchester-Bromley area
Mad River Glen, Waitsfield
Merck Forest Foundation
Mountain Top Inn, Chittenden
Prospect Mountain, Woodford
Putney
Stowe—Mt. Mansfield Toll Road, Summit Trail, Long Trail, North Cemetery Trail, Kidder Brook Jeep Trail
Swedish Ski Club Lodge, Andover
Winter Bivouac, Northfield

MIDWEST
Illinois:
Palos and Sag Valley Forest Preserve

Wisconsin:
North Kettle Moraine State Forest
South Kettle Moraine State Forest
Lake O'Brien, Upson

Michigan:
Brule Mountain, Iron River
Cannonsburg, Cannonsburg

Grand Haven Ski Bowl, Grand Haven
Iroquois Mt. Lodge, Sault Ste. Marie
Lost Pines Lodge, Harietta
Missaukee Mountain, Lake City
Mt. Frederick, Grayling
Mt. Mancelona, Mancelona
Porcupine Mountain, Ontonagon
Skyline, Grayling
Snowshake Mountain, Claire

NASTAR Nordic Touring Centers

Alaska:

Alaska Ski Touring Center
Alyeska Ski Area
Seward Highway
Girdwood, Alas. 99587

Colorado:

Scandinavian Lodge
Steamboat Springs
Colo. 80477

Illinois:

Norge Ski Club
Fox River Grove, Ill.

Maine:

Sugarloaf Mountain
Kingfield, Me.

Minnesota:

North Star Ski Touring Club
Jonathan, Minn.

New Hampshire:

Dana Place
Box 95
Jackson, N. H.

New York:

Glens Falls Cross-Country Touring Center
Crandall Park
The Inside Edge Ski Shop
253 Bay Road
Glens Falls, N. Y. 12801

Ohio: *The Ski Haus Ski School, Inc.*
                         12417 Cedar Road
                         Cleveland Heights
                         Ohio 44106

Oregon: *Mt. Bachelor*
                         Bend Ski Touring Center
                         Route 3, Box 450
                         Bend, Ore. 97701

Vermont: *Woodstock Ski Touring Center*
                         Woodstock Country Club
                         P.O. Box 483
                         Woodstock, Vt. 05091

                         Mt. Snow
                         Mt. Snow, Wilmington, Vt.

                         Burke Mountain
                         Lyndonville, Vt.

                         Sugarbush Inn
                         Sugarbush, Vt.

Washington: *Mission Ridge Ski Center*
                         Box 542
                         Wenatchee, Wash. 98801

Wisconsin: *Sunburst Ski Area*
                         5856 N. Port Washington Road
                         Milwaukee, Wisc. 53217

Annual Events

Washington's Birthday Tour: (Vermont) Oldest and largest regularly run tour race in the United States. For information, write Race Committee, Putney School, Putney, Vermont 05346.

Madonna Vasa: (Vermont) Held on first Sunday in March to coincide with the Vasa in Sweden (the 85 kilometer classic). For information write Dr. John Bland, Upper Valley Road, Cambridge, Vermont 05444.

Stowe Derby: (Vermont), Starts at Handy's West Hill in Stowe and you can either run a course of two and one-half or nearly seven miles. For information write Jack Handy, Stowe School, Stowe, Vermont 05672.

Canadian Marathon: (near Montreal) Covers 80 of the 100 miles of the Montreal-to-Ottawa trail, and takes two days. It's open to racing or touring single runners, two-man teams, four-man teams and juniors, as well as mixed age and sex teams. Usually held late in February. For information write the Viking Ski Club, P.O. Box 57, Morin Heights, Quebec, Canada.

V-J-C Ski Tour: (Minnesota) Course starts in Victoria, goes through Jonathan and ends in Chaska (ergo: "VJC Tour"). Event is held in late February. For information write North Star Ski Touring Club, 4231 Oakdale Avenue, Minneapolis, Minnesota 55416.

The Gold Rush: (Colorado) Starts near Breckenridge, 10,000 feet up on the Continental Divide, finishes 10 km later at Summit County High School in Frisco. For information write Frisco Chamber of Commerce, Frisco, Colorado 80433.

Yosemite: (California) Ten km race. Write to Yosemite Mountaineering School, Yosemite National Park, California 95389.

John Craig Memorial: (Oregon) Run by Oregon Nordic Club. Named after John Craig who helped build by hand the first road across McKenzie Pass, and carried mail across it during winter. In honor of him, each racer carried mail during the race, which goes over the pass, east to west, and averages 18 miles total. For information write Ed Park, Bend Chapter, Oregon Nordic Club, Bend, Oregon 97701.

Fairbanks Skiathon: (Alaska) Twenty km over the Sharland Ski Trails; the race is held around March 20th to coincide with the vernal equinox. For information write Nordic Ski Club of Fairbanks, Fairbanks, Alaska 99701.

Glacier Stampede: (Alaska) Course starts halfway between Fairbanks and Anchorage on the Richardson Highway, climbs 8 miles up Cantwell Glacier to an Alpine cabin. Each skier has to carry a tent, sleeping bag and provisions for the overnight stay. Held at end of April. Write Nordic Ski Club of Fairbanks, Fairbanks, Alaska 99701 for information.

Keystone Cross Country Caper: (Colorado) Held at Keystone Ski area for the first time February 13, 1972, sponsored by the Keystone ski area and Scandinavian Airlines. For information write to Robert L. Hall, Race Chairman, Keystone Ski Area, Keystone, Colorado.

Bibliography

Ski touring and racing

Brady, Michael. *Nordic Touring and Cross-Country Skiing.* Oslo, Norway: Dreyers Forlag, 1970.

Brady, Michael and Kristen Kvello, *The Norwegian Training Program, Men's Cross-Country.* Oslo, Norway: Norwegian Ski Association, 1965.

Caldwell, John. *The New Cross-Country Ski Book.* Brattleboro, Vermont: The Stephen Greene Press, 1971.

Casewit, Curtis. *Ski Racing: Advice By The Experts.* New York: Arco Publishing Co., 1969.

Lederer, William J. and Joe Pete Wilson. *Complete Cross-Country Skiing and Ski Touring.* New York: W. W. Norton & Co., 1970.

Kjellstrom, Bjorn and Bill Rusln. *Ski Touring for the Beginner.* LaPorte, Indiana: Silva, 1972.

Osgood, William E. and Leslie J. Hurley. *Ski Touring, An Introductory Guide.* Rutland, Vermont: Charles E. Tuttle Co., 1969.

Ski Touring Council, Inc. *Ski Touring Guide.* New York: Ski Touring Council, Winter 1968-69.

Wahlberg, Jack. *Cross-Country Skiing, Touring and Racing.* The Swedish Amateur Ski Association, Montreal, Canada, (Silva, Inc.)

Related topics

Ald, Roy. *Jogging, Aerobics and Diet.* New York: Signet Books, New American Library, 1968.

Angier, Bradford. *How To Stay Alive in The Woods.* London: Collier Books, Collier MacMillan Ltd., 1969.

Atwater, Montgomery M. *The Avalanche Hunters.* Philadelphia: Macrae Smith Co., 1968.

Benjamin, Dr. Bry, and Annette Francis Benjamin. *In Case of Emergency.* Garden City, New York: Doubleday & Co., 1965.

Brander, Gary. *Living Off The Land*. Los Angeles: Nash Publishing, 1971.

Brower, David, Ed. *The Sierra Club Manual of Ski Mountaineering*. New York: Ballantine Books, 1969.

Cooper, Dr. Kenneth H. *Aerobics*. New York: Bantam Books, 1969.

Cunningham, Gerry, and Margaret Hansson. *Light Weight Camping Equipment*, Fourth Edition. Denver, Colorado: Colorado Outdoor Sports Corp., 1968.

Fraser, Colin. *The Avalanche Enigma*. London: Published for John Murray, by William Clowes & Sons, 1966.

Fredericks, Dr. Carlton. *Great Eating For Weight Watchers*. New York: Award Books, 1968.

Herbert, April. *The Tailgate Cookbook*. New York: Funk & Wagnalls, 1970.

Hunter's Encyclopedia Staff. *Camping and Camp Cookery*. New York: Collier Books, 1962.

Kjellstrom, Bjorn. *Be Expert With Map and Compass*, New Revised Edition. LaPorte, Indiana: American Orienteering Service, 1967.

Lachapelle, Edward R. *The ABC of Avalanche Safety*. Denver, Colorado: Highlander Publishing Company, Colorado Outdoor Sports Corp., 1961.

Mendenhall, Ruth Dyar. *Backpack Cookery*. Glendale, California: La Siesta Press, 1966.

Mendenhall, Ruth Dyar. *Backpack Techniques*. Glendale, California: La Siesta Press, 1967.

Mountaineers Climbing Committee. *Mountaineering: The Freedom of The Hills*, Second Edition. Seattle: The Mountaineers, 1969.

Nesbitt, Paul H., Alonzo W. Pond, and William H. Allen. *The Survival Book*. New York: Funk & Wagnalls, 1968.

Stephens, Mae Webb and George S. Wells. *Coping With Camp Cooking*. Harrisburg, Pa.: Stackpole Books, 1966.

Cross-Country Ski Touring Films

The following films are supplied free to ski clubs or other organizations on request.

Ski Touring is For People:
By Paul Ryan and Morten Lund for Garcia Ski Corp., 100 Galway Place, Teaneck, New Jersey 07666. This film includes ski touring instruction, touring sequences, and deep powder skiiing on tour skis (12½ minutes, color).

Silent Skis:
G. H. Bass, Bass Sports, Inc., Box W., Wilton, Maine 04294. A lyrical evocation of touring (20 minutes, color).